Tuesday's PERSPECTIVE

GROWING FORWARD, ONE TUESDAY AT A TIME

Jennifer Kay Koger

Tuesday's Perspective
Growing Forward, One Tuesday at a Time
Jennifer Koger

Contact the author
jkkreflections@outlook.com

Published and Edited by:

Mary Ethel

Mary Ethel Eckard
Frisco, Texas

Library of Congress Control Number: 2025919885
ISBN (Print): 978-1-966561-27-9
ISBN (E-book): 978-1-966561-28-6

CONTENTS

ACKNOWLEDGEMENTS

I want to thank my husband for being my biggest supporter and my children for always believing in me.

To the three ladies who helped me get this book off the ground, thank you for walking alongside me and cheering me on every step of the way.

To the woman who inspired me to write this book and stood by my side throughout the process, your presence made all the difference.

And most of all, I thank God for never leaving my side, and for trusting me to be obedient to His guidance.

FOREWORD

It is with deep joy and gratitude that I write this foreword for Jennifer's book. I first met Jennifer when she came to me, seeking guidance through the Twelve Steps, with a heartfelt desire for a better marriage and to regain a sense of calm and control. From our very first conversations, her dedication and relentless pursuit of solutions were evident. She felt like a victim, but she also knew she was contributing to the problem in ways she had not yet recognized. She didn't shy away from the conflicts she experienced with her husband, children, or coworkers; instead, she approached them with a unique blend of honesty and an unwavering commitment to growth. Although it was not always graceful.

What truly sets Jennifer apart is her deep reliance on God and her unflinching honesty. This honesty forms the bedrock of her transformation and the journey she shares in *Tuesday's Perspective*. These reflections, which she so openly shares with God and her friends, are a testament to her journey of self-discovery and spiritual deepening.

Working with Jennifer has been a profound gift to me. Her insights and perspectives have often illuminated new paths for my own spiritual journey, helping me to see situations with fresh eyes and a renewed sense of purpose. Her courage to face challenges head-on and her unwavering faith have been a constant source of inspiration.

I do not doubt that you will find Jennifer's book as insightful, relatable, and transformative as I have. Her words are not just reflections; they are an invitation to examine your own life with honesty, seek solutions with an open heart, and lean on a power greater than yourself. I hope you love her book as much as I do.

With all my love,
Brandy

INTRODUCTION

This book is a collection of my reflections, written on Tuesdays, usually early in the morning before the world fully wakes up and life demands my attention. I called it *Tuesday's Perspective* because that's precisely what it is: my honest, unfiltered thoughts on life, faith, family, recovery, and everything in between—on a regular Tuesday.

It started as a way to connect. I began writing and sending these messages to a small group of women, many of whom I met through recovery, church, or just life. It was my way of saying, *"You're not alone in what you're going through, because I'm walking through it too."* Over time, what began as texts or emails turned into a rhythm—a spiritual practice, almost. Every Tuesday became a sacred space for honesty and growth.

Writing *Tuesday's Perspective* helped me sort through the noise in my head and the emotions in my heart. I wrote when I was hurting, when I was hopeful, and even when I was angry or confused. I didn't always know where the words would lead, but somehow, they always helped me come back to the truth: that God is still with me, I am still growing, and grace still covers all of it.

These pages are not about having it all figured out. They are about the process. The wrestling. The surrender. The joy that sneaks in unexpectedly. And the healing that comes—sometimes slow, sometimes sudden—when we tell the truth.

If you've ever felt like you were the only one trying to make peace with your past, or hold your family together, or rebuild your faith, I hope something here reminds you that you're not alone. I hope my honesty permits you to be honest too—with yourself, with God, and with the people you love.

Most of all, I hope you leave these pages feeling seen. Encouraged. And maybe even a little more willing to show up for your own story.

—JKK

A Glimpse Into My Story

Good morning, Friend,

Here's a little bit about me: I was born in Dallas in 1979. I have four older siblings and three younger siblings on my dad's side, though I don't know the younger ones. On my mom's side, I have an older half-brother and a younger brother. They grew up with me.

I didn't attend school very often. If I add it all together, I probably attended about three years total, as far as I can remember.

I've been married twice. I have three children, each with a different father, and two bonus children that came with my husband, making a total of five kids.

I'm also a grandma! I have one grandchild and two more on the way.

I have been clean for seven years. My clean date is January 1, 2016.

I live in Texas, and I *love* Jesus.

One of my favorite things to do in the morning is share pieces of my heart and story with *you*.

Today I am grateful for:

- The woman I am today, because of everything I've been through.
- My clean date—and every clean day since.
- A God who loves me exactly as I am.

What parts of your story have shaped who you are today—and how can you honor them?

What are you grateful for today?

A Few of My Favorite Things

Good morning, my beautiful friend.

Here are a few things about me:

- My favorite color is turquoise.
- My favorite rose is called a JFK.
- I like getting up early, usually between 5:30 and 6:00 a.m.
- My grandparents had a huge garden when I was growing up, and I learned so much about life in that garden.
- My favorite coffee is made by *me, anything with ch*ocolate.
- My favorite meal is calamari, steak, a salad with balsamic vinegar, and a baked potato.
- My favorite fruit is pomegranate. I believe that wherever heaven is, God will have a pomegranate tree waiting for me, with the best pomegranates I've ever tasted.
- I love trying different restaurants, but I'm not a fan of sushi or most fish.
- My favorite movies are Wh*at Dreams May Come a*nd The *Shack.* I also enjoy crime and action movies, though I've been trying to cut back on crime shows—they give me nightmares.
- When I'm by myself, I still sleep with a small light on. Part of me is still afraid of the dark.
- I enjoy taking pictures of clouds and the ocean.
- I love my friends, and I'm working hard to love others, even when we don't always get along.
- The best part about being a mom is *everything.* And being a grandma? Even more fun!

That's a little bit about me. How about you?

Today I am grateful for:

- The garden where I first learned about life.
- Pomegranates and the promise of heaven.
- A heart that keeps learning how to love.

What are some of your favorite things—and what do they say about who you are becoming?

What are you grateful for today?

Staying Put Isn't Always Easy

On Monday, my husband and I were not in the best place. I attended a meeting, didn't look for a divorce lawyer, and didn't create a Tinder account. **Recovery is working.**

I talked with my sponsor about wanting a new, more prestigious job, and about quitting my service position at my Home Group. Her words were: *"You need to stay at this job for at least a year and stop bouncing around. And you need to fulfill your service commitment because it is a commitment."* Her words pissed me off.

She's right, though.

I'm struggling with letting God take care of my kids and keep my marriage healthy, even when I know I have no control.

Reality really feels heavy.

Have a great evening.

Today I am grateful for:

- My job, because they treat me like I'm a person.
- My husband, because even when we're mad, we still sleep in the same bed, kiss each other goodnight, and say I *love you.*
- My sponsor, who doesn't mind telling me the truth, even when it hurts.

Where in your life are you tempted to quit—but maybe, just maybe, you're supposed to stay?

What are you grateful for today?

Enough as I Am

Good afternoon, Friend,

I've been struggling with control lately, and my biggest issue has been around what people think of me, especially what my boss thinks of me.

Even when I work hard and do my best, I still feel this need for her to validate my worth. I go back and forth in my mind about whether I belong in this company. But the truth is, I am *me* — and today, that is enough.

So instead of looking to her for approval, I'm going to focus on what's in front of me right now… which happens to be reviewing insurance benefits.

Today I am grateful for:

- The ability to recognize when I'm seeking outside validation.
- Steady work that allows me to provide for my needs.
- God's reminder that who I am today is enough.

How would your day feel different if you fully believed your worth didn't depend on anyone else's opinion?

What are you grateful for today?

Myself

I've been hanging out with my thoughts a little too much this week.

Here's a little more about me:

- My favorite time of day is when I get to see my family.
- I believe Heaven is me and Jesus being in the same place at the same time.
- I care what people think of me—until I stop being self-obsessed.
- It takes a lot for me to start trusting someone.
- Sometimes I live in the past because it's familiar, and not all of it was bad.
- I like to fantasize about the future—sometimes to the point of fear.

Today I am grateful for:

- The freedom to be myself without pretending to be someone else.
- The progress I've made in recovery since 2016.
- God's patience with me when I fall back into old ways of thinking.

When you get caught up in self-obsession, how can you redirect your thoughts back toward gratitude and God?

What are you grateful for today?

Fixing Him

This morning, my husband said he needed to find a place he could attend regularly to clear his head. Immediately, my thoughts went to: *How can I fix this for him? I should invite him to my home group so he can finally see what it is like.* But here's what I know deep down: I tell myself I want to help him change, but the truth is, I don't want him to be around places where he might get to know other women on a personal level. Because if he does, he might leave me.

Let's be honest. I'm not responsible for his life and decisions. Trying to control what my husband does in his life only sets me back in my recovery, especially when it comes to trusting God and trusting myself.

So just for this moment, I'm going to step out of God's way. I'm going to allow myself to let go. Letting go is hard. But it's necessary—for both of us. I can recover.

Today, I'm grateful for:

- The opportunity to let go of control
- Not being the one in control
- Not having to fix him

Are you helping because it's truly loving, or because you're afraid of losing control?

What are you grateful for today?

Check-In

Job

Today, I have a phone call with an area manager from a property in the city regarding a sales position. We'll see how it goes—God's got me!

Husband

We had a fantastic date night on Friday. Lingerie was the way to go! Breakfast at a Pancake House was so good.

Children (Grown-ups)

I have so much more peace when I don't try to fix their problems or tell them how to live.

Children (at Home)

They're doing well in school, and they've gotten a little more sarcastic these days. They got it honestly.

Recovery

I only attended one meeting last week and missed my home group on Tuesday. I won't be able to go this week either because we're having people over for Halloween. I plan to do more online meetings this week and attend a couple in person as well.

And if nobody's told you today, I love you. I love you. Have an amazing day.

Today I am grateful for:

- For cold days—they remind me how much I appreciate the warm ones.

- For the opportunity to share my life with you, knowing you never judge me.
- I get to break my fast with *chocolate c*offee at 9 a.m.

What are you doing this week to stay connected to your recovery while balancing life's responsibilities?

What are you grateful for today?

Self-Obsession

It's Monday again, and I'm sitting at the doctor's office waiting to hear what the next steps are for my son.

Husband

I'm learning to step back and allow my husband to go through his process.

Kids (Grownups)

They're doing what they need to do for their own lives.

Friends

I'm still a little sad that a female friend I once had doesn't want anything to do with me. But I'm getting to practice acceptance.

God

I love God, and I'm still learning to trust Him.

Self

Lately, I've been caught up in self-obsession—so much so that my sponsor gave me an assignment. What I'm learning is that it's not other people's responsibility to fix my insecurity or make me feel liked. I like to tell myself I don't care what others think about me. But the truth is, I care a lot—so much that I try to make people see me a certain way.

That behavior wears me out. Being myself is so much better than being the version of me I *think* someone else wants.

Thank you for being you. Have a blessed week, my friend.

Today I am grateful for:

- The relationships I've had with people, even if they were only for a season.
- Who I am, whether I'm with someone or standing alone.
- What God thinks about me.

Are you willing to trust that who you truly are is enough?

What are you grateful for today?

Letting Go or Holding On

My boss and I were able to resolve the issue. Our meeting yesterday went well—she shared that my lack of trust in her had hurt her feelings. She also told me that my job means a lot to her because I work hard, I'm trustworthy, and she relies on me to do the right thing.

As for my obsession over whether my husband is lying, it's caused harm to our relationship. He told me it hurts him that I don't trust him, and that my behavior sets us back every time.

I'm starting to see a theme here. This all comes down to *me not trusting God*. The truth is, I don't know how to feel… okay. For example, nothing is going wrong; life is simply doing what life does. And yet, I either *let go and let God*, or I keep choosing *not to* be okay.

Thanks be to God for His patience—and for His clarity.

Today I am grateful for:

- A boss who values and affirms my work.
- The willingness to see patterns in my behavior.
- God's patience as I learn to trust Him fully.

When nothing is actually wrong, why do you still struggle to feel okay?

What are you grateful for today?

Letting Go of the Case

Good morning, Friend,

Today, my son has surgery, and my husband and I are not speaking—unless necessary. I woke up still angry from yesterday, tempted to go searching for evidence of him on social media and convince myself he's lying about something.

My mind immediately starts coming up with reasons why he *would* lie.

What am I really worried about? Here I go again, taking an inventory of *his* recovery. I catch myself thinking, *He's not doing what he needs to. He's not calling his friends. He's not doing the things I want him to.*

But the truth is—*his* life is *none* of my business. So, what can I do instead of building a case against my husband? For starters, I can stop thinking about *myself* and be present for my *son.* That's precisely what I'm going to do.

God has allowed me to show up and be of service to our son, and I'm going to trust God to take care of my husband.

Have a blessed day.

Today I am grateful for:

- The opportunity to be present for my son during his surgery.
- Awareness of when I'm slipping into control mode.
- God's gentle reminders to trust Him with the people I love.

How might your relationships change if you focused on your own recovery instead of taking inventory of others?

What are you grateful for today?

Catching You Up

Our middle son made it through surgery and is recovering well so far. Last time, the nurses had to pry him off of me—he was terrified to go into the operating room. But this time, he looked back and simply said, *"I love you, y'all."*

My husband and I are still a little fussy with each other. But most of our disagreements only last a couple of days now. There was a time when they would've lasted months. One of the hardest things for me is to give him space when he asks for it. I'm still working on that one.

My oldest son seems to be doing well—*just for today.* He's working and showing up even when he doesn't want to. This time around, Michael and I had him sign a living agreement before moving in. Boundaries in action.

Being a wife, mom, sister, daughter, aunt, and friend means making hard choices that don't always feel good. But recovery and boundaries are teaching me to offer myself the same patience I ask God to give others.

Love you to the moon and back. Have a great day!

Today I am grateful for:

- My oldest son
- The people who go to school to learn how medications work
- Hard relationships—they're where the growth happens

How can you give yourself the same grace and patience you're learning to give others?

What are you grateful for today?

Instant Family

Good morning, Friend,

A friend shared with me this morning about the struggles she's facing—financial pressures and the weight of being a single mom. Our conversation brought me back to the time I asked God for a husband with children—someone to share life with.

Not long after my husband and I got together, he gained custody of both of his children. And just like that, I had an instant family. I had to learn how to live with someone *and* his children. It meant letting go of the old "my way or the highway" mindset. Because I've lived a lot of my life that way… and the highway got very lonely.

I also learned to ask God to help me not only love my husband, but also to love his children as if they were my own. I'm grateful for the reminder today.

Have an amazing Tuesday.

Today I am grateful for:

- The family I never expected but deeply needed
- A softer heart that chooses love over control
- God's faithfulness in answering prayers—even when the answers require growth

What prayer from the past are you living in the answer to today?

What are you grateful for today?

Work in Progress

Good morning, my Friend,

I came into work today, and, of course, my computer is doing its thing when it needs an update. Typical, right?

I've been facing some struggles in my marriage lately, and I'm hoping we can get into counseling soon. My husband has a trip planned to New York in December, and I've been grappling with a range of emotions about it. Communication in my relationships hasn't always been a strong point for me, but I'm hoping marriage counseling will help us both grow.

I can't be upset with my husband for doing something I initially said yes to—especially when I didn't take the time to fully process how I felt before agreeing. Then I catch myself getting mad at him later, when the truth is… I'm still a work in progress.

I'm currently reading *Tradition Seven* and living out *Step Six*.

Please have a great one, my beautiful friend.

Today I am grateful for:

- The moments where I can reflect on my actions.
- My husband.
- This day.

How often do you say "yes" before truly understanding how you feel about the situation?

What are you grateful for today?

Bravery and Prayer in
the Waiting Room

Good morning, Friend,

Today, my son had surgery on his left foot. Honestly, I wasn't sure if I'd even be able to make it to the surgery center. I was sick yesterday and all through the night—my body couldn't hold down food or water. But this morning, I prayed… and I pushed through.

My son was so brave, even though just before he was taken back for surgery, he broke down and cried. I watched as his bonus dad—his stepdad—held him close.

I witnessed our son get so nervous that he didn't even want to speak. And in that moment, God pulled me out of how I was feeling so I could be present for him.

Before surgery, the nurses asked our son if he wanted to pray, and he said yes. So, there we were—my husband, two nurses, and our boy—gathered together as one of the nurses prayed out loud over him.

When they rolled him back, he cried for me. I promised I would be right here when he woke up. And I will be.

I'm so grateful to have a relationship with God. But even more, I'm thankful that *my son* has a relationship with Him, too. He's learning that being brave doesn't mean you're never scared.

Being brave means you *are* scared
    and you do it anyway,
Because it's the right thing to do,
    and you know God is in control.

Today I am grateful for:

- The strength to show up for my child despite being sick.
- Nurses who pray with their patients.
- Watching my son build his own relationship with God.

When was the last time you had to be brave, even though you were scared?

What are you grateful for today?

Character Defects and Grandbaby Love

Good morning, Friend

Today is my first grandbaby's first birthday. Time has flown by so quickly. I look at my children and sometimes wish they were still little—that I could do it all over again. Then, after spending two or three days around them, I'm thankful they're adults!

The thing about being a grandma is that my children now get to raise their kids how they want, and I no longer get a vote. My grandmother was my very favorite person, and my great-grandmother came in second until I got a little older. Then my grandpa was my second favorite person. I hope my grandchildren feel the same way about me someday.

The gifts God has blessed me with are more than I ever thought to ask for. And let's be honest, I look good for a grandma in her mid-40s! I'm also *not* conceited at all. This is probably why I'm currently working on Step 6—character defects and all.

Today I am grateful for:

- The joy of being a grandmother.
- The role models my grandparents were in my life.
- The opportunity to grow through Step 6.

What character defect are you most ready to release so you can fully embrace the blessings in your life?

What are you grateful for today?

Gratitude

Today, I'm reflecting on the simple yet powerful things I'm grateful for:

- I am grateful for boundaries, even when it hurts to stand in them.
- I am grateful for cell phones that let me stay connected with my people.
- I am grateful that there is so much more to me than my looks.

Wishing you a well-blessed evening, my friend.

How can you pause in your day to notice and appreciate the small, ordinary gifts God has placed in your life?

What are you grateful for today?

Craving Health

Good evening, Friend,

I've spent the last 48 hours wondering when I'll finally be able to eat without getting sick. Tonight, I took my chances with a bit of beef broth and a glass of water. I've been sipping both slowly—still a little scared I won't be able to hold it down.

There is truly no amount of money or riches that compares to the wealth of *health.* My husband mentioned how pale my face looked today, and the funny thing is—I didn't particularly care.

Right now, I'm craving the most random things: pickles, candy, even pizza. And if you know me at all, you know I *never* crave pizza. Until now.

It's been a few years since I've felt this bad, so today I'm especially grateful for the gift of health—and for the fact that, most of the time, I *am* healthy.

Side note: My son is doing great after his surgery!

Today I am grateful for:

- Warm broth and cold water.
- Resting without guilt.
- My son's recovery going smoothly so far.

How often do you pause to appreciate your health—especially when you're feeling well?

What are you grateful for today?

Love That Stays

Good afternoon, Friend

Today, I'm proud of who I am—and the fact that I was able to stay home all weekend by myself and not use. That's a victory worth celebrating.

I shared part of my journey with others on Saturday, and now I'm sitting at the animal hospital because my dog ripped his nail. I can see how much pain he's in, and I couldn't let him keep suffering.

I have so much more love in my heart today than I did seven years ago when I got clean. The truth is, I'm still here and present in my life because God never left me—even when I turned my back on Him.

Today, I can laugh at things I used to take personally. For example, one of the nurses just asked my dog Mac, "How are you not sleeping with the medication we gave you? Or at least lying down?" And all I could think was—*he's probably an addict and has a high tolerance!*

I love this dog—even when he gets on my nerves and runs under the bed.

Recovery isn't easy, but it is *so* worth it.

Today I am grateful for:

- Seven years of recovery and the ability to laugh at life.
- My dog Mac and the unconditional love he brings.
- God's constant presence in my life.

What small victories in your life are worth celebrating today?

What are you grateful for today?

Heels Against the Wall

Today, I'm grateful that I can walk. I couldn't walk until I was three years old because a part of my foot didn't develop properly when I was born.

At age five, I was told I'd likely be in a wheelchair by the time I turned thirteen—that I'd struggle to walk, and that there was no corrective surgery for my condition. I remember sitting on the edge of that exam room bed with my feet dangling. I looked up at the doctor, and my mom and I said to them, "I will not be in a wheelchair because Jesus has things for me to do.

So, I did what I could.

For what felt like years, I spent 30 minutes a day, three times a day, with my toes on a phone book and the backs of my heels pressed against a wall. I had to put in the work from the very beginning. And God did the rest.

Since that diagnosis, I've been able to walk every single day.

I'm sharing this with you because it's one of the many things in my life that have made me stronger.

Have an amazing day.

Today I am grateful for:

- A mother who believed in me and pushed me to fight.
- The ability to walk freely—even when it once seemed impossible.
- A God who gives me purpose, even in my pain.

What are you grateful for today?

Weight Loss

Good morning, Friend,

I've been doing this fasting thing—14 hours of fasting and a 10-hour eating window—for the past eight days. It's not easy. I obsess over what I'm going to eat the second my fast ends. But like anything else in my life, I must ask God for help through the entire process.

I'm tired. I'm hungry. I'm impatient.

And let's be honest—I haven't been able to drink black coffee. (Because... *yuck*.)

I want to lose weight and feel better—physically and mentally.

I've tried all kinds of diets and pills in the past — anything to avoid the hard work of changing my behavior.

Remember the walking journey I started a couple of weeks ago?

Yeah... I stopped after a few days.

But with fasting, my hope is that I'll stay consistent, and that eventually, other good decisions and healthy habits will follow.

One day at a time.

Have an amazing Tuesday.

I love you, my beautiful friend.

Today I am grateful for:

- The willingness to try again
- God's strength when mine runs out
- The hope that healthy change is *possible*

What's one area of your life where you're ready to trade shortcuts for real change?

What are you grateful for today?

When Life Looks Sunny
and Feels Stormy

Good morning, Friend,

Today, my two younger boys are coming home from church camp. I'm so excited to pick them up and hear all about their trip.

Meanwhile, the computers are down at one of the properties I manage. I've been fasting every day, trying to improve my physical well-being. Both of my daughters are expecting baby girls.

I'm working on my part in my marriage.

I have a relationship with God that I know needs to be nourished.

And still—somehow—I find time to obsess over what my grown son or my mother is doing… or not doing… according to *my* standards.

There is so much going on in my life right now. And when I start to feel overwhelmed by *my* life, I've noticed something: That's when I start focusing on everyone else's life—the parts I wish I could control. Meanwhile, mine is quietly spinning out of control.

Only on the *inside*, though…

Because on the outside?

Everything looks sunny and bright.

Today I am grateful for:

- My boys returning home safely.
- A God who meets me in my mess.
- The awareness to recognize my old patterns before they take over.

When life feels chaotic, do you tend to focus on yourself—or try to fix someone else?

What are you grateful for today?

My Messy Day

I have made a mess today. Let me explain.

Work

My boss had to kindly ask me—again—to stop bringing up my job position. She said if anything changes, she'll let me know. Then, I spilled a whole cup of coffee all over myself *and* my office. And all of this happened before 9 a.m. To top it off, I went to a job interview at a hotel where they told me I wasn't qualified for the current openings. However, they encouraged me to keep their contact information because I'm smart and heading in the right direction.

Recovery

I've been obsessing over how to control the outcome of my current situation. I'm powerless over outcomes, and honestly, I've been causing some pain to those around me—both at work and home—because I struggle to accept the answers I've been given.

Husband

We went to counseling, and so far, we're still married. I don't have a new apartment picked out with a deposit ready to go… although, if I'm being honest, those thoughts still cross my mind. Total fantasy, though.

Kids (Grown-Ups)

I still don't get a vote in their lives. I know my kids have good hearts, and one day, they'll recognize their worth. I'm proud to be their mom.

Kids at Home

They're currently grounded. And one of them managed to earn themselves an extra week. Now, we, as parents, are grounded right along with them.

Have a thankful week. Love you, friend.

Today I am grateful for:

- My family
- The people I work with
- Shampoo

How can you accept the answers you've been given without trying to control or change them?

What are you grateful for today?

When Forgiveness Isn't Instant

Good evening, Friend.

I haven't texted anyone about what's been going on in my life the past few days. Honestly, I've been feeling sorry for myself.

I didn't get a raise at work. Then a friend told me she's still not over something I did that hurt her *two years ago.* At the time, I had no idea I had even hurt her. And once I found out, I asked what I could do to make it right. Today, she let me know she's not ready to rebuild our friendship. She said she felt abandoned by me.

I've been walking around for days feeling *not good enough*, and today, that message seemed to be confirmed. But I've managed to keep my emotions in check—with God's help, of course.

I've also had to remind myself:

My worth is no*t b*ased on my job.

And it's no*t b*ased on whether someone forgives me or not.

My purpose is to love others, love God, and show up as the best version of myself — one day at a time.

Today I am grateful for:

- My job.
- Friendships, both the ones that are thriving and the ones that are healing.
- A God who reminds me of my value, even when I feel unworthy.

Where have you been placing your worth? Is it time to shift that focus?

What are you grateful for today?

Becoming Who I Was Meant to Be

Today, I had one phone interview and one video interview with two different companies. There was a time in my life when I didn't believe I was worth much of anyone's time. I masked those insecurities with arrogance and self-righteousness. I've worked hard to get and stay clean—to become a better mom, friend, wife, and employee.

I earned my GED and a degree in hospitality, yet I still didn't believe I deserved to be fully present in my own life. But life itself — living it, feeling it, walking through it—has taught me so much. I've learned who I am, who I'm not, and who I want to become.

Today, I understand that the destination matters, but so does the journey it takes to get there. And in the middle of it all, I feel unconditionally loved by my best friend, Jesus.

Have a wonderful evening.

Today I am grateful for:

- The chance to show up for job interviews with confidence.
- The growth that came from hard lessons.
- Jesus' unconditional love.

What parts of your journey have helped you become someone you're proud to be?

What are you grateful for today?

Loving From a Distance

Good morning, my beautiful friend.

Yesterday was my mom's birthday, and I didn't see her, even though she lives only three miles away. I had to force myself to send her a text that said, "Happy Birthday, I love you."

The relationship between my mom and me hasn't been great these past few years. I forgive her for everything, and I hope she forgives me. Still, when my mom says hurtful things, I tend to forgive her, step back into her life… and end up getting hurt all over again.

Yesterday was the first time I was able to fall asleep without feeling guilty for not being more present in her life.

She doesn't text or call me unless she's feeling guilty—or wants to say something hurtful. People say things like, *"She's your mom, and she won't be around forever. Do everything you can to be in her life."*

I used to believe that having a relationship with my mom was solely my responsibility. But God, the program, and the process have taught me that not all relationships are healthy, and that it's okay to have boundaries. I love my mom, and I always will… even if that love must come from a distance.

Today I am grateful for:

- The courage to love someone from a distance.
- Healing that doesn't require permission.
- The strength to choose peace over guilt.

What boundary have you set that honors both your healing and your love for someone else?

What are you grateful for today?

Letting Go and Showing Up

Good afternoon, Friend,

Today, my emotions have been all over the place.

I woke up feeling sad and anxious about a situation that hasn't even happened yet—and may never happen. But if it *does*, I still won't have any control over it.

If I'm being honest, that's probably what I'm sad about: *not having control.*

Despite how I was feeling, I still showed up to work on time, which, yes, is something I *should* do anyway. But today, it felt like an emotional victory.

Later that morning, my boss told me she's working on getting me a raise.

Now, I don't value myself by how much money I make—but I must admit, it felt terrific to hear that I'm valued as an employee.

For those who know me well, you know Jesus is my best friend. And I truly believe He used today's praise as a loving distraction from my desire to control someone else's life.

So, if you're in a place right now where you need to hear how much you are loved and valued—I'm telling you now: I value you. I love you.

Have a great day.

Today I am grateful for:

- The ability to show up when I'd rather shut down.
- A boss who sees my value and speaks it out loud.
- A God who redirects my focus with gentle, loving reminders.

Where in your life are you trying to control an outcome that God is asking you to release?

What are you grateful for today?

A New Generation of Love

Good morning, Friend,

Today is a wonderful day—my daughter had her baby girl! She weighs 6 pounds, 7 ounces. Her name excites me because it reflects my middle name.

Being a grandma at 44 is something I once thought would make me feel old, but instead, I feel *blessed*.

This morning, I get to go to work. I have friends and family who genuinely care about me. My children have allowed me back into their lives. *This* is what living looks like for me today. Living clean is so much better than the alternative.

Have a fantastic day.

Today I am grateful for:

- The joy of welcoming a new granddaughter into the world.
- Restored relationships with my children.
- The gift of living clean and present in the moment.

How can you be intentional about showing love and presence to the next generation in your family?

What are you grateful for today?

Healthy Boundaries at Work

I made a huge mistake by sending my boss all the personal text messages I usually send to you. Even though I asked her if she wanted to be a part of it and she said yes, I shouldn't have shared to the level of honesty that I did.

The truth is, I only asked her because she was struggling with feeling accepted by other women, and I identified with her pain. I wanted her to feel accepted, but that wasn't my responsibility. That's where I crossed a line. She's not an addict or a close friend, and moving forward, I must stop treating her like one.

Now, I'm obsessing over what I shouldn't have done. Please pray that I can stop behaving in a way that makes me appear immature or not ready for a higher position. I struggle so much with acceptance and not feeling good enough.

Lately, I've also been worried that my company will eliminate my position because the owners are selling the property. And honestly, I've put my career at risk to feel better in the moment, to feel connected or validated.

From now on, I'm going to treat my boss like a boss—with respect and healthy boundaries, not like a close friend. The hard part is stepping back, letting the chips fall where they may, and allowing God to take care of it. I'm powerless over whether the company gets rid of my position. I'm even powerless if they let me go.

But what I *can* do is grow, change, and move forward.

Have a great week, my friends.

Today I am grateful for:

- For not having all the answers.
- That life is not always easy.
- For the experience.

How can you create healthy boundaries that protect both your professional relationships and your emotional well-being?

What are you grateful for today?

Walking In With My Head High

Good morning, Friend,

Today I get to go to my interview, and I'm nervous—or maybe a better word for it is *excited*. I'm still riding the pink cloud from making it through the weekend by myself and trusting my husband to be faithful. I avoided everything that could have dragged me into a negative mindset, and that feels like real growth.

But I do have to be careful with that pink cloud. Sometimes I convince myself that because I made it through alone, I don't need or even want to be with my husband.

I've also been feeling some emotional pain about my older children living their own lives and not having any control. But today, I'm going to keep the focus on *me*. I'm walking into this interview with my head held high, knowing God's got me, and He's got my kids, too.

Today I am grateful for:

- The opportunity to interview for a new position.
- Growth in trusting my husband and myself.
- God's care over my children, even when I'm not in control.

Where in your life do you need to walk forward with your head held high, trusting that God has it covered?

What are you grateful for today?

Right Where I'm Supposed to Be

Good morning, Friend,

Today, I am grateful. I'm feeling under the weather with a sore throat and not much energy, but my heart is whole.

The interview went great. I'm not in a rush to leave the people I work for, though. I've gotten used to my work family, and they've become a special part of my routine. Still, I trust that God will take me wherever He wants me to be. I also believe that I am successful, *right now, in this moment.* I'm working hard to be the best version of myself and to stay present in my own life.

Lately, I've had the opportunity to sit with some complicated feelings that come with having such a beautiful family. It's not always easy, but it's worth it.

Thank you for allowing me to share my life with you. Thank you for being *you*—for believing in me, checking on me, and just being there when you don't hear from me.

My relationship with you is truly a gift.

Today I am grateful for:

- A successful interview and the peace of trusting God's plan.
- The gift of my work family.
- Relationships that bring encouragement and support.

Where in your life can you slow down and appreciate being right where you are?

What are you grateful for today?

Figuring Out the Lesson

Good morning, Friend,

Yesterday at work was super busy, and it felt like I couldn't keep up. Even though I wasn't feeling well, God gave me the strength to push through the day, and I even managed to make chicken salad after I got home.

My older brother is still not talking to me. Maybe that's a blessing… I'm just not sure what the lesson is yet. I keep telling myself, *he's the one who said people who go to the rooms are losers, and they should've been doing the right thing all along, so they don't deserve to be rewarded for it.*

Now, he didn't directly call me a loser—but that's what it sounded like to me. Maybe I should tell him how that made me feel. I also need to remember that he felt like I was attacking his character, and that's what started this sibling quarrel in the first place. He reacted from a place of hurt because he misunderstood something I said. And here I am… doing the same thing. There it is. I think I just figured out the lesson. I need to let God work this out and stop trying to fix it.

Have a terrific Tuesday.

Today I am grateful for:

- God's ability to reveal lessons in the middle of conflict.
- The strength to get through a busy workday even when I don't feel my best.
- Chicken salad waiting for me at home.

When misunderstandings arise, are you willing to pause and let God work in the situation instead of rushing to fix it yourself?

What are you grateful for today?

Letting Go In Love

Good morning, Friend.

I've been so busy the last few days that I haven't sent out a "sharing my day" text. So, where do I start?

We had the baby shower yesterday, and on Friday, I went to a screening with John Cusack. That was cool because I had the biggest crush on him when I was a little girl. He seemed humbler than I expected.

I've always had this idea that famous people think they're better than me, like, why would someone like that ever talk to me? But the truth is, they have more money than I do. It's not fair for me to judge them, especially while I'm judging myself at the same time through comparisons. That's a cycle that doesn't serve anyone.

On a different note, the baby shower went well. Still, it hurts a little— my daughter doesn't seem excited about her baby. I've come to accept that the best and most important thing I can do in this situation is to pray... and let go.

Today I am grateful for:

- Time spent celebrating new life.
- The reminder that comparison is a trap.
- Peace in letting go of what I cannot control.

Where in your life do you need to release control and simply love the best you can?

What are you grateful for today?

Unplugged

---✦---

I've been unplugged from my people. Today, I want to share where I am.

Work

I've stopped oversharing with my boss. I've started treating her like a boss again, not a confidante. I have a job interview today at a resort, and for once, I'm not spinning out of control about my current job. That's progress.

Recovery

I went to my home group meeting, even though my face was broken out, and I didn't feel great about how I looked. I went anyway.

Husband

Last night, I had a dream in which I kissed another man. In the dream, I was miserable trying to figure out how to tell my husband. I felt so ashamed and disappointed in myself. I woke up and was thankful to be lying next to my husband, realizing it had just been a bad dream.

Older Brother

He texted me a while back, but he still won't answer my calls. I keep calling, still hoping he'll pick up one day.

Mom

We're still talking, and I'm learning to accept her for who she is, while also learning to accept myself in the process.

Grown Children

They're still living their lives, making their own choices. Right now, I'm not trying to save them. My oldest son turns 23 this month.

Kids at Home

Our middle son got his stitches out, and our youngest is finally ungrounded. They're growing up so fast. These clean days of mine have truly been the best days of my life.

Have an amazing day.

Today, I'm grateful for:

- Antibiotics
- Doctors
- The ability to be responsible for my life

What relationships or situations could become healthier if you simply accepted them as they are today?

What are you grateful for today?

Life Without My Permission

Good evening, Friend,

It's been a heck of a few days. I've been going back and forth about whether to look for a new job. My daughter is having her baby tonight. My oldest son has a lot going on in his life. My youngest has had a fever for a couple of days. My husband is working two jobs. And my second-to-youngest is having surgery on the 6th. With everything going on, I've decided to stop chasing another job and trying to control the outcome of all these situations.

A very special lady once told me, "If you really trust God the way you say you do, then step out of the way—because life is going to be life without your permission." She was right. Life is a lot more peaceful when I live in acceptance.

Have a great evening.

Today I am grateful for:

- Wise words from people who have walked before me.
- The peace that comes from acceptance.
- God's steady presence in the middle of uncertainty.

Where in your life are you still trying to control the outcome instead of trusting God?

What are you grateful for today?

When Emotions Text First

Over the weekend, my older brother told me we're no longer family—and then he blocked me. That hurt.

I can own my part. I texted him things that should have been said face-to-face. I've learned that when I let emotions drive my texting, it never ends well. That behavior—reacting instead of responding—has cost me relationships. I also let what my mom says affect how I interact with others. Instead of brushing off her comments, I repeat them to the person she talked about, creating more tension. The pattern keeps repeating—and I see it now.

Tonight, I celebrate eight years at my home group. I'd be lying if I said I wasn't nervous about what others might say. But I'm also incredibly grateful for the process, for the growth, and for the chance to take an honest look at myself.

Have an awesome day!

Today I'm grateful for:

- Pomegranates that are still in season.
- People who care enough to listen—and tell me the truth.
- My grandbabies smiling just at the sound of my voice.

What emotional habits are you ready to let go of—and which ones do you want to strengthen?

What are you grateful for today?

Examining My Part

Husband

Today my husband and I are going to counseling, and I am practicing *not* bringing my semi-automatic emotional weapon to fire shots that prove how right I am and how wrong he is. I must really examine my part. A lot of our communication issues come from me agreeing to things I'm not truly okay with—and then getting upset at him for doing the thing I agreed to.

Children (Grown Up)

They're living their lives the way they choose. Sometimes it's painful to watch, but I am blessed that they're still in my life and that I get to be their mom. One of the greatest honors in my life is being called *Mom*.

Children (at Home)

They're growing so quickly! I feel like both will hit puberty at the same time—they're 10 and 11 (almost 11 and 12). For anyone who's gone through this preteen stage, please keep us in your prayers.

Work

I'm thankful for my job, and I hope to continue growing within the company.

Mom

She and I have been on good terms lately. If you knew what our relationship used to be like, you'd understand what a miracle that is. I'm letting go of expectations—both for her and for myself. I feel like I'm finally heading in the right direction.

Older Brother

He texted me that he's not mad at me and that he loves me. I'm not sure he even realizes that what he said felt like he was calling me a loser. We haven't talked yet, but we are moving forward.

Friends

I have friends—and I love them. I'm so blessed to be someone's friend today.

Recovery

Yesterday, I was in the *"F** them steps and spiritual principles"* kind of mood. But today is a new day. Yesterday's recovery isn't enough for today.

Love you, my friend. Have an awesome week.

Today I am grateful for:

- Family.
- The things I sometimes complain about, because I forget how blessed I am.
- The good and the bad—and my shifting perception of them.

Are you willing to take a fearless look at your part before pointing out someone else's?

What are you grateful for today?

Changes—Inside Out

These past seven days have been rough on me and the people around me. I've started the process of coming off my antidepressants. I didn't realize how much of my emotions were being suppressed by the medication until now.

No need for alarms—I'm under a doctor's care *this time*.

No more operating under "Jennifer's medical advice."

Yesterday, I spun out for a while and started believing my husband was cheating on me. I almost left work to drive by the place he was *allegedly* supposed to be. But I started praying, and God stopped that runaway train before it tore down my marriage.

Still, I caused some harm. My husband said he forgives me, and he's here for me.

The shame and guilt hit hard when I got home. I wanted to lie in bed and hide my face from the world. Instead, I got up, cooked dinner, and watched a show with my boys while my husband was clearing his head.

I hope that I get to know *myself* without the antidepressants—and that I still like who I find. I hope other people like the Jennifer I'm working on becoming, too.

Yes, I'm afraid—afraid I might not be able to get off the medication, fearful of who I'll be without it.

But I have *hope*.

I want you to know that I'm here for you, and I'll walk with you. Thank you for being part of my support group and walking with me, while God continues to change me from the inside out.

Have an amazing day.

What I like about myself:

- I can be honest with myself and with you, once I see the problem.
- Instead of calling everyone to cry and complain about my husband yesterday and today, I reached out and asked how *they* were doing.
- When the emotional waves started to crash inside me, I finally turned to my God for a solution, rather than to people, places, or things.

What part of yourself are you learning to meet with grace instead of fear?

What are you grateful for today?

Staying Out of God's Way

Good morning, my Friend,

Today, I'm feeling a little better. Last night, I had to tell my son that he couldn't stay the night. My husband and I have agreed on some boundaries: if our grown children are going to continue living the lifestyle they're living, they can't stay the night or live with us. Even though we set that boundary together, I was mad at my husband yesterday for sticking to it when it came to our oldest son.

This morning, I read a page from some literature about detaching from addiction—and wow, it hit me. I am so addicted to my children and so codependent on their love for me. Letting go and letting God is going to require a strength that doesn't come from me. I've allowed my children's choices to control my peace and my mood for far too long. So today—once again—I'm practicing staying out of God's way.

Today I am grateful for:

- The strength to hold firm to healthy boundaries.
- A husband who stands with me in tough decisions.
- The reminder to let go and let God.

What boundaries do you need to honor today, even when it's hard?

What are you grateful for today?

Being a Brat!

Good morning, Friend,

Today I'm super busy again—which is incredible—but I acted like a spoiled brat at the tire shop this morning. I got there before they opened and waited in my car, assuming that, like other tire shops I've been to, someone would come out to help me. That wasn't the case. No one came to my car.

So, I went inside and asked—probably with a bit of an attitude—if it was normal not to assist the people who pull into the parking lot first, or if you're supposed to stand in line. The gentleman inside responded very kindly and took the time to listen to my concerns. Then another man came over and spoke to me with grace and patience. That's when I realized what a brat I was being.

I apologized for assuming how their process worked and thanked them for helping me. For the rest of the day, I'm going to practice using kind words—or not saying anything at all.

Have an amazing week!

Today I am grateful that:

- People tell me "no," and I get to learn how to be okay with it.
- My job gave me the time this morning to get my tire fixed.
- I had the money to fix it.

How often do you react based on assumptions instead of taking a moment to understand the situation?

What are you grateful for today?

Hope Shot: Thanksgiving

I attended my meeting and, on the way home, I called my husband to discuss Thanksgiving. He told me he didn't want to be a part of it this year.

By the time I hung up the phone, I had already convinced myself our marriage was over, just like that. It's wild how quickly I go to the extreme. If someone—especially my husband—isn't acting the way I expect, I immediately start writing the ending. I can be such an all-or-nothing thinker.

So, I called another recovering addict and started crying. I told her and her husband, who were both on the phone because of Apple CarPlay, how I felt disrespected, unwanted, like my husband didn't care about me anymore. I told them I should probably leave. My friend's husband gently said, "Maybe just wait until your emotions settle. You recently stopped taking your antidepressants."

That was hard to hear, but it was true. It's been less than a month since I stopped taking them, and my brain's still adjusting. They prayed with me. I went to bed.

Wednesday

My husband and I made plans to visit his son's mother's side of the family for Thanksgiving. I was curious to see how this *Jerry Springer Family Thanksgiving* (My Life) episode would play out.

Thursday – Thanksgiving

It turned out to be a great day. I thought I'd feel uncomfortable and jealous, but I wasn't. God was with me the whole time, and I was unapologetically myself. I trusted and believed in my husband that day, in his commitment to our kids and our marriage.

I sat close to him. I showed him affection in front of others. I took tons of pictures and posted them because I was proud of who I am today.

We ended the day driving to Oklahoma to pick up our daughter, but she wouldn't come out of the house to get in the car. We waited, then left. I did get to stop by Choctaw for a bit, which was cool, although we weren't there long, and I left smelling like a Marlboro factory.

Friday

My husband went Black Friday shopping with our son while I worked. One of our boys had a fever, and I wasn't feeling great either—but strangely, I was happy.

Saturday

All but one of our children came over (our daughter stayed in Oklahoma). We had Thanksgiving lunch. It was *so* fun. My little brother came, and my older brother—who hadn't spoken to me in almost a year—unblocked me. I knew this because my message finally showed as "delivered." Two of our three grandbabies were there. It was a beautiful, blessed day.

I wish I could explain how everything in my life and marriage seems to have undergone a complete turnaround. What I *can* say is this: I absolutely believe it started the night my two friends and I prayed together.

All week I had a sore throat, stuffy nose, and could barely breathe— but I smiled, I laughed, and I stayed in the moment more than I have during any holiday season in years.

I wasn't even going to write a *Tuesday's Perspective* this week. Someone asked me if I was sure I was sharing this with people who had my best interests at heart.

Here's the truth: people are going to people. I'll never really know who's rooting for me—and who isn't.

But I share anyway.

If someone takes what I say and uses it against me, I can't control that.
I live out loud in the hope that what I've gone through—and how I tell
it—might help someone else, even if I never know who they are.

God gave me a gift: self-awareness and the ability to put my life into
words others can relate to.

That, right there, is a hope shot.

Today I'm grateful for:

- My family—all of them Whether they're using or not, speaking
  to me or not—I love them
- Knowing how to follow directions when cooking chicken and
  dressing and still remembering how to make my grandma's
  homemade banana pudding
- The people who reached out asking, "Where's this week's *Tuesday's
  Perspective?*"

Have a happy Thanksgiving.

**What's one moment this week that surprised you with peace or joy—
when you didn't expect it?**

What are you grateful for today?

New Job

I recently started a new job, and while I genuinely enjoy it, I've been wrestling with some old feelings of insecurity. Thoughts like, *"Am I smart enough?"* have been creeping in, especially when I catch myself worrying about my grammar.

It's hard sometimes, wondering if the people I work with can see the insecurities I still carry from not having had the opportunity to go to school growing up.

But here's the thing:

I'm showing up. Every single day.

I'm doing my best, and I'm learning to remind myself that growth takes time.

I've come this far because of the relationships I've built and the resilience I've grown along the way, with the help of God, and that's something to be proud of.

Wishing you a beautiful day filled with gratitude and peace.

Today, I am grateful for:

- My health.
- My children, who remind me why I keep striving.
- The journey my husband and I are on—learning to love ourselves and each other more deeply.

How can you focus on showing up and giving your best, instead of letting insecurity steal your peace?

What are you grateful for today?

Believing This Time Will Be Different

Good afternoon, Friend,

I keep doing this thing where I want to believe *this time will be different*—and each time, it hurts more than the time before. I think about what I could have done differently and promise myself I won't let it happen again... *(until I do)*. Without even mentioning the other person's part, I can confidently say they have good intentions. But they're not the one I need to focus on changing.

I am the one who needs to change. And that truth applies to more than one relationship in my life.

Today I've cried, felt frustrated, been sad, laughed, and even cleaned. I spent two hours playing a board game with my younger boys—while living the *real* game of life at the same time. Today has been painful.

Have an amazing day!

Today I am grateful for:

- Hot showers.
- Tears.
- Every single one of my feelings.

How many times will you keep hoping others will change, before you finally allow God to change you?

What are you grateful for today?

Seeking Approval

Today I'm on-site doing training at my new job. Last week, I spent the first few days seeking approval from someone who isn't even in my inner circle. This time, it only took me a couple of days to realize that I *am* likable, and I don't have to feed my addiction to insecurity by people-pleasing.

Thanksgiving was good. I got to spend time with my in-laws and didn't get too offended—so I call that a win.

I also met my niece and nephew from my younger sister's side of the family for the first time. My good friend of 15 years drove up to San Antonio, and we all ate at Steak. Two of my grown children and two of my grandchildren were also there.

Being clean from my addictions has given me a life full of family, friends, and God.

Have a great day, my friend.

Today I am grateful for:

- The free coffee I got today.
- My husband.
- My family and the beautiful mess that my life is today.

Whose approval are you still chasing, and what would happen if you let go?

What are you grateful for today?

A Season of Shifts

This past week has been a whirlwind of emotions.

Relationships:

Let's start with my marriage. Things have calmed down, and I haven't felt the urge to find reasons to leave. My emotions aren't driving all my decisions anymore. That's growth.

Our middle daughter has started calling me for advice—*what?!* This is the same child who, in the past, would've done something wrong a hundred times before ever asking for my help. The only downside is she now thinks I have all the answers. Still, I must admit—it feels incredible to be seen like a superhero by the one child who once seemed to hate me the most.

Work:

I prayed to book this group at the property—we needed the business. So, when I received the email saying they had chosen another property, I was disappointed. I had to break the news to my boss that the bid was lost. Things at work do not look the way I want them to in terms of revenue and numbers.

But here's something I'm proud of: I stopped trying to take business from the mentors who once trained me at a previous job. If I'm being honest, I was trying to hurt them the way I felt they hurt me. But that only backfired—and it pulled me out of character. Now, I'm praying for something better. I'm asking God to send *me* clients—the ones meant for me—and to bless the people I once tried to compete with out of pain.

Health:

Right after I got that disappointing email about the lost bid, the doctor called with the results of my CT scan. I held my breath. Then the voice on the other end of the phone said, "Your scans are clear."

I was overwhelmed with joy and gratitude. I had already started planning my funeral, figuring out how much it would cost, wondering if I should increase my life insurance so my husband wouldn't be left with the bills. I tend to go to the worst possible outcome of any situation. The phone call from the doctor's office brought me back to reality.

Holiday Season:

I put up the Christmas trees—both at home and at work. That's new for me. Usually, I could take or leave all the Christmas cheer. But I haven't taken an antidepressant since November 14th, and I didn't want to believe that something so small—one pill a day—could change me that much, but it did.

I'm singing Christmas music. I'm cooking more. I'm judging my family less and accepting things for the way they are. The best part of it all? I'm finally enjoying my feelings, not running from them. I'm not taking life *so* seriously every moment of every day—and I'm giving myself a break.

Have a fantastic week!

Today I'm grateful for:

- Being able to attend our son's 7th-grade Christmas concert.
- The gift I received from work—Brand name perfume and lotion.
- All the fun and ridiculous Christmas music that lifts my spirit.

What's something you've recently let go of that's made space for peace or joy in your life?

What are you grateful for today?

Hope. Confidence. Commitment.

Hey you!

Today I worked, and I was grateful for all the changes. I'm 44 years old and still learning. Honestly, the more I learn, the more I realize how much I don't know.

For this year, I've chosen three words to guide me: **Hope**, **Confidence**, and **Commitment**.

For the past five years, I've made it a practice to pick a word—or a few—to focus on throughout the year. I'm not big on New Year's resolutions; they usually don't stick. But I *can* practice living out a few words each day, to the best of my ability. That's helped me accept that I'm human—and that it's okay to give myself a little grace.

When I used to make resolutions—such as "eat better" or "lose weight"—I'd often end up not meeting my expectations. Then I'd spiral, start disliking myself, and fall into self-pity. These three words? They're a gentler, stronger way forward.

Have a fantastic night!

Hope – to look forward to something with desire and reasonable confidence.

Confidence – complete trust; belief in the powers, trustworthiness, or reliability of (God).

Commitment – the act of pledging or engaging oneself fully.

Today I am grateful for:

- God's gentle reminder that His love is bigger than my fear.
- The ability to pause and resist my old pattern of rescuing.
- Peace, even if just for today, knowing the outcome is in His hands.

What words do you want to carry with you into the next new year?

What are you grateful for today?

Turning Harm Into Good

Good morning, my Friend,

Today marks day five of waking up early to get my boys on their school schedule. School officially starts on Wednesday, and I'm genuinely thankful that they can meet new people and experience new things.

Man, I miss my two older children being little. I spent too many years not being the mom I am today. Still, I believe that the things they've been through—because of my addiction—will shape them into who God wants them to be.

Now, don't get me wrong—I'm not saying they *deserved* a mom who put drugs, men, and money above them. What I *am* saying is that the God I trust takes the things meant for harm and turns them for good... even for an addict like me.

Today I am grateful for:

- The opportunity to be present for my children today.
- The way God redeems even the most painful seasons of life.
- The joy of seeing my children grow into who they're meant to be.

How has God used your past mistakes to create something good in your life today?

What are you grateful for today?

Giving Thanks for All of It

If I told you I was happy with every area of my life, I'd be lying to you and myself.

But I *can* say this: I am content in this moment.

I found out the doctor doesn't believe I have cancer. I still have one more test to go—a CT scan with that iodine stuff they inject into your veins. You know, the one that makes you feel like you must pee and your whole body warms up? That happens on December 9th.

Am I scared of the results? Not too much right now. Mostly because my mind is elsewhere, wondering if my husband still really wants to be married to me. Wondering if I'll *ever* feel secure enough not to worry that he might cheat on me. Wondering if I'm even good enough. These insecurities are heavy.

But I'm thankful to *have* these concerns and character defects—because that means I'm still alive and clean.

My husband has told me he's tired of my insecurities. He said he's going to be himself, and if I can't trust him to have an appropriate conversation with a woman, without having to explain every detail, then I can leave.

> I don't believe he's cheating.
> I don't believe he wa*nts t*o cheat.
> I believe he wants me to trust him.

Then there's my 12-year-old son. I saw a text he sent to a girl:

"Why won't you talk to me anymore? What did I do? I need you and don't know what to do without you. Please talk to me. I'm about to cry."

Reading that broke my heart. Because it sounded just like me... texting his dad. I went to my son and apologized for how I've acted. I told him he learned that behavior from me, and I want to change that, and I can with God's help.

I told him that *if someone ignores you, won't respond to you, or says they don't want to be around you, respect that. Move on. And don't you ever beg someone to love you. You're worth being loved. When we beg people to notice us, it crushes our self-esteem and feeds theirs.*

Was that the right thing to say? I don't know. I'm doing the best I can, and I don't have all the answers.

Lately, I've even found myself wishing someone would call my husband and tell him how wrong he is and how much he's hurting me, because my husband does not hear me when I say it.

But I've decided:

> I'm going to focus on me.
> I'm not going to fall into the trap of needing to be needed.
> I'm not going to live in my insecurities.
> Because I mu*st* change if I'm going to be the parent my children need.
> Will I do it perfectly?　Not a chance.
> Will I backslide sometimes? Absolutely.
> But when I fall, I'm going to fall forward.

Hug your family. Hug your friends. Hug *yourself.*

Today, I'm grateful for:

- My perspective.
- My marriage.
- Clarity.

What belief or behavior are you ready to unlearn—for the sake of who you're becoming?

What are you grateful for today?

Showing Up for Myself

Today, I get to take care of myself by visiting the doctor for a follow-up blood test and a medication review. Switching mood medications has been an emotional roller coaster, but things are finally starting to level out.

Most of what I'm thinking about this morning is how I need to hurry up at this appointment so I can get to work and stay busy. I remember the days when I was constantly trying to find reasons *not* to go to work and still get paid. I'd use any excuse: calling in sick, saying I needed to take care of something for my kids or my mom. That behavior was rooted in my addiction.

When I got clean, I discovered that I'm actually a hard worker, and I'm *grateful* for the ability to provide for my family.

Life is different today. I love you. Have an amazing day.

Today I'm also grateful for:

- For showing up on time—no longer trying to weasel out of doctor appointments or work.
- For my home group meeting every Tuesday night.
- To have insurance right now, even though some days I resent how much I have to pay each month.

What's one way you've surprised yourself with growth lately?

What are you grateful for today?

From Approval to Awareness

Good morning, Friend,

A lot is going on in my adult children's lives right now. I'm struggling with knowing the difference between *being there* for them and *enabling* bad behavior. Sometimes, those lines feel so blurred. What helps is when I slow down and focus on *how* I'm feeling, and when I don't know how I think, just being still. That stillness keeps me from reacting out of disease.

For example, at my last job, I constantly sought my boss's approval. I wanted to be the *best* at everything, and I forgot that my worth wasn't tied to her opinion of me. I had *lots* of practice at that job on what *not* to do.

Fast forward to my current job. Just yesterday, I texted my boss and didn't get a response right away. My mind went straight to, "I'm going to get fired. She doesn't like me. I'm not good at this job." But instead of acting out of insecurity, I waited. And waited. *For hours.* Eventually, she texted me back. She *thanked* me for asking before just doing something and told me to have a good day.

There's still that little girl in me who's searching for her mother's approval in every woman I meet. I want to blame my mom for that insecurity. But here's the truth: I'm an adult now. And my mother did the best she could, whether I want to believe that or not. She was a single mom. She made mistakes, but she loves me.

Today, I get to take responsibility for *my* actions. I get to own my part. And I get to move forward.

Have an amazing day.

Today I'm grateful for:

- Having a mom—because not everyone does.
- Trusting myself enough to trust my husband more than I used to.
- The women in my life who've shown me what it means to be a woman.

Where in your life are you still seeking approval—and what truth can set you free from it today?

What are you grateful for today?

A Simpler, Saner Way

I've been living in my Step Nine—and I'm learning to let go of unnecessary tasks I create that only add stress to my life.

For example, I have a planner that breaks down goals by day, week, month, and quarter. Somewhere along the way, I picked up a made-up belief that I *have* to fill out every single line—part of my weird thinking. I got into the solution, though.

I got a new planner—just lines to write on—
starting July to July. Simpler. Saner.

I've recently gone through a medication change, and the withdrawal from my old antidepressant has been *rough*, to say the least.

I'm starting to wonder if I have ADHD—I can't seem
to finish one task without starting another.

I've been more irritable and less compassionate lately.

I'm so ready for my brain to level out.

Still, my life is full of blessings,

Even when I don't recognize the wrapping on the present.

Have a great day.

Today I am grateful for:

- For conflict and for the ability to seek solutions instead of staying stuck.
- I'm not playing doctor this time and trying to quit my meds cold turkey.

- For learning more about myself, my patterns, and my part in the amends process.

What's one thing you've complicated that could be made simpler, with grace and honesty?

What are you grateful for today?

Paradise Redefined

I've been on a cruise since Saturday, and my idea of "paradise" has shifted since last Tuesday. I used to think paradise meant lounging on a turquoise beach with white sand, sipping a virgin piña colada. Don't get me wrong—those things are beautiful, and I still enjoy them—but lately, I find myself missing my adult children, my grandchildren, and my mom. I even miss my brothers (yes, even the one who doesn't want to talk to me).

The dictionary defines *paradise* as "a place of extreme beauty, delight, or happiness," and even "heaven." Now, I believe paradise is being surrounded by people I love and who love me back. I believe the God I trust is at the center of that love. Paradise is seeing the good, even when everything around and inside me feels chaotic and ever-changing.

Have an amazing night, my friend.

Today I'm grateful for:

- A God whose mind never changes, even when mine does.
- The space and permission to grow—and to fail—as I learn.
- The color green (it's everywhere on this ship!), and the fact that I turn 45 this coming Sunday.

What's your version of paradise today—and how has it changed from what you once believed?

What are you grateful for today?

Loving People Where They Are

I've lost a couple of pounds—learning how to eat things that are better for me.

My youngest daughter has been visiting more frequently lately. She's even called me for advice on how to handle certain things.

I'm learning how to parent my adult children in the present, without holding them—or myself—stuck in the past.

My husband went out of town for work this morning, and I haven't felt the urge to check his location or log into our cell phone account to see who he's called.

That's what freedom from active addiction feels like.

I met my oldest sister for the first time this past Sunday. I'm 45 now. I didn't think I would cry, but I did. Even after 44 years, I felt an immediate connection.

Letting God control the timing—and not trying to force my siblings to meet me—was the right choice.

Have a wonderful evening.

Today I'm grateful for:

- For my little sister from my dad's last marriage. She was the first to accept me and meet me before any of the other siblings, including the one I met on Sunday.
- For DNA kits that connect you with family online. Because of the people who created that platform, I've been able to reconnect with my siblings.
- Even though the older brother I grew up with still wants nothing to do with me, I can *still* find joy in the hope that one day,

things could change. I can love him where he is—without chasing him through emails, social media, or phone calls. I respect his decision… and I've given it to God. It took a while, though, because I emailed and called him.

Where in your life are you learning to let go—and love people right where they are?

What are you grateful for today?

I Wouldn't Have Believed It

Let me start by saying—my new boss called me *awesome* yesterday. It might not have meant much to her… but it meant something to *me*.

My kids are doing well. My husband and I are still together. And even if this moment doesn't last forever—*man*, I'm enjoying it while it's here. I forgot how fun I can be. I forgot how often I take myself *way* too seriously.

It's almost time to board the cruise ship. And honestly—eight years ago, if you had told me I'd be married… with a family… living in a home… raising my kids… working a job I (sometimes) enjoy… and *liking* myself on top of all that—I would've laughed in disbelief. I wouldn't have believed it was possible.

But here I am.

Have a fantastic day. And if no one's told you today: *I love you.*

Today I'm grateful for:

- You believe in me—even when I don't.
- Learning how to love myself.
- Living in the moment.

What's one part of your life today that your past self never would've believed was possible?

What are you grateful for today?

Still Grieving

Good morning, Friend,

Yesterday marked 21 years since my son passed away. Although I lost him at birth, I spent years blaming myself for his death. I had placenta previa, and both my son and I were pronounced dead at 10:28 p.m. on June 19, 2001.

This is the story I've been told—I don't know all the details of what happened between the time I was pronounced and when they realized I had survived. But I remember so much of that night as if it were yesterday.

While I was in the hospital, I prayed constantly. I prayed that God would take my son, whom I was pregnant with, home. It's painful to say, but I prayed that prayer because I knew if I gave birth to him, his father would try to kill me if I ever tried to leave and take our son with me. I was trapped in a highly abusive relationship, and I couldn't see any way out.

On the way to the operating room, I was praying out loud:

"God, please don't let the living son's dad get him. Please put him in a good home where he will be cared for."

I was thinking of my oldest son's dad. I don't even remember praying those words, but that's what the doctors told me later.

So, as I was facing death, the only thing I could think about was the safety of my *living* child. I woke up in an empty hospital room, confused, not understanding what had happened. Eventually, the nurses brought my baby to me, wrapped in a white blanket.

He was still. He was gone.

I held my breathless son in my arms, and though I was heartbroken, I was also… grateful. God answered my prayer.

A few days later, I came home. I had to find a ride back to my house from the hospital because I couldn't reach my boyfriend. And when I got home, I walked through the door, and I found another woman in my bed.

That moment could've destroyed me. But it didn't.

I'm so incredibly grateful for the life I live today—and for everything God has brought me through.

Today I am grateful for:

- The strength to survive what should have destroyed me.
- The memory of holding my son, even if just for a moment.
- The life I live today—one that God is still shaping with grace and healing.

How has God met you in the midst of your pain—and what has He brought you through that you never thought you'd survive?

What are you grateful for today?

Choosing Myself Anyway

This morning, I'm choosing to like myself. Yesterday, my boss told me they're going to keep moving forward with me, for now. She said once I get written up enough and fail to improve, they'll let me go. She also told me I need to decide whether I even *want* to work for this company. And right before the call ended, she said, *"I've never had to deal with anyone like you."*

That one stung. But today, I'm not letting what someone thinks of me keep me down. I have reviewed my actions repeatedly, and I still don't know what I'm doing wrong in this job.

I know the ground is level at the foot of the cross, in the rooms of recovery, and yes, even at my job. I don't believe my worth is based on whether someone likes me or not. I *do* admit that sometimes my insecurities get the best of me. They affect my mood, my actions, and I hand people the power to define me. But I don't stay in that "poor me" space for very long anymore.

Thank God for the opportunity to learn the lesson. Have an amazing day, my beautiful friend.

Today I'm grateful for:

- Taking my power back.
- The people who speak life into me.
- Being able to accept that I'm not a good fit in everyone's life, job, or relationship.

Whose opinion have you been giving too much power—and how can you take that power back today?

What are you grateful for today?

The Pattern Beneath the Pressure

I've had all this turmoil building up inside me over this job situation. I was called into the office for a two-hour meeting on Friday, followed by a 30-minute meeting on Monday morning, and then received a lengthy email from my boss on Monday evening listing all the things I was doing wrong.

I shut down on Friday. I gave up on trying to make this job work. I started slacking on my responsibilities, and I even took a half-day off yesterday, convincing myself that it didn't matter what I did because there was no saving this job.

I even disguised one of my actions—opening a new bank account—as doing what was best for my group. But the truth is: I don't know what's best for the group.

A friend pointed out that what I'm going through at work feels a lot like how I felt growing up with my mom. That's something I need to take a deeper look at.

I was able to respond to my boss's email with grace, letting her know that I didn't believe I was a good fit for this position and that I would begin looking for another job. In the meantime, I committed to working on meeting her expectations. No slacking on the job today.

Have an amazing day.

Today I am grateful for:

- Owning my part.
- The job interviews I've gone on over the past three days.
- Having a Higher Power who's willing to help me, and who seems to help even more when I admit my part and take the steps to make things right.

**Where in your current life are you reliving an old emotional pattern—
and what would it look like to heal that part of your story now?**

What are you grateful for today?

Butterflies and Goalposts

Good morning, Friend,

Today is the championship game for my boys' soccer team. They're at that age where half the time they're focused on the game, and the other half, they're chasing butterflies or hanging from the goalpost.

But watching them fall, get back up, and rejoin the game—no matter what happens in the first or second half—is *inspirational*. They remind me that whether they're stopping to enjoy the butterflies or giving it their all to score a goal, life is about living fully and embracing every part of it.

And when life knocks you down? Get back up.

Because your team, whether that's your family, friends, or coworkers, still needs you.

Today I am grateful for:

- The playful spirit and resilience of my boys
- The reminder that joy and purpose can coexist
- A team—on and off the field—that counts on me

Where in your life do you need to get back up and rejoin the game?

What are you grateful for today?

The Cost of Being Liked

I got written up on Friday for not doing my job well enough. They told me I have until February 13th to make the necessary changes. One of my bosses told me that I need to make sure the people I work with *like* me, because if someone doesn't like me, I'll be out.

The funny part? That's one of my biggest struggles: people not liking me. Right away, my mind started planning how to win everyone over. I came up with all these ideas about how I'd change myself—put on a little fake here and there—to keep my job.

But deep down, I know that's not the lesson I'm supposed to be learning. The lesson is to be *myself*, to do my best at work, and to trust that God will take care of the rest.

I'll be honest—sometimes even when I say I'm giving things to God, I'm still secretly plotting and scheming in the background, trying to control the outcome. Letting go isn't easy.

Being myself is one of the hardest things to do… because I *want* everyone to like me. But every time I change who I am to keep someone or something I think I deserve, I go against my values. And when things *don't* work out the way I hoped, I end up resenting myself. That resentment often shows up as anger toward the person, place, or thing I was chasing in the first place.

The truth is, I may not get to keep this job. But I *can* be myself. I *can* do my best. And I *will* trust that God's got me.

Have a fantastic day!

Today I'm grateful for:

- A God who loves me exactly as He made me.
- The opportunity to learn how to love—and li*ke*—*m*yself.
- The people in my life who support me and help me grow in that love.

Where are you tempted to shrink, shape-shift, or overperform just to be liked—and what would staying true to yourself look like instead?

What are you grateful for today?

Practicing the Stay

Yesterday, I had a meeting with my boss about my performance. I may lose my job soon. Right now, I'm sitting with fear, insecurities, and those old, familiar feelings of *not being good enough.*

It's hard to stay put when everything in me wants to run—to avoid the pain of being let go. But today, I'm practicing something different: staying. Even when I don't want to.

Thank God for His power and His constant presence—even in the hard times. I'm not running from life today. Whatever happens will happen. And sometimes… things just don't work out the way I hoped.

Have an amazing day!

Today I'm grateful for:

- The opportunity to do what's *right,* even when walking away would be easier.
- The awareness that my self-esteem gets stronger when I stay true to my character.
- The difficult people I've met, worked with, lived with—including myself.

What part of your life is calling you to stay, even when everything in you wants to run?

What are you grateful for today?

A Note to Myself

Good morning, Friend,

Today, I'm still struggling with trying to control how people feel about me and what they think of me. I want the people I work with to *like* me. This morning, I asked the general manager at one of my properties if I could spend some time with each employee—perhaps even conduct some training—because there are so many moving parts, and I enjoy getting to know my team.

Her response was, "The most patient people will be these two." Then she gave me two names and followed it with, "Other than that, I don't have anyone you could train with." Ouch.

The harder I work to do a good job, the more I feel *less than*. This codependency—this need for approval and validation—is kicking my butt today. Why is it so hard for me to accept that if people at work don't like me, or if people in general don't, it doesn't mean I'm not doing my job. It doesn't mean I'm not worthy.

So, Here's my note to myself this morning:

Jennifer, kn*ow your worth*. Have acceptance for yourself today.

Have a great day.

Today I'm grateful for:

- Understanding that I'm human.
- The sound of God's voice in the middle of the chaos in my head.
- Healthy lunch bowls from my favorite lunch spot this month. (Yes, really!)

What truth do you need to remind yourself of today—especially when others' opinions try to define your worth?

What are you grateful for today?

When Work Becomes the Higher Power

This past week, I haven't been very present with my children or my husband because I've been trying so hard *not* to lose my job. I haven't gone to enough meetings. I haven't picked up my step work. And the result of neglecting my recovery has been… devastating.

I've been yelling at my kids, arguing with my husband, biting my nails, and—worst of all—I stopped listening to God. I made my job my Higher Power and put *myself* in the God seat.

Today, I'm recommitting to my recovery. I will do the best I can at work, but when I get home at 5 p.m., I'm committing to being *present* with my family. I'll go to more than just one meeting a week. I'm choosing to be okay with *myself*, and I'm choosing to trust God again.
It amazes me how quickly I fall back into the habit of putting my job before everything else. I did that in active addiction. And I've learned that it causes harm to my family, to myself, and to everything I love.

I've missed too many important moments in my children's lives already because I've made other things look like they mattered more. I can make it *look* like I'm doing the right thing, but deep down, I know when I'm out of balance.

Have a great day, my friend.

Today I'm grateful for:

- A husband who is understanding and walks with me through my trials.
- The women in my life who check on me when they haven't heard from me.
- The opportunity to share my life with *you*.

What have you accidentally started worshipping—and what would it look like to trust God with it instead?

What are you grateful for today?

Clarity & Letting Go

I've had some clarity over the past seven days. I emailed my older brother to invite him to Easter lunch, and I had no expectations of him responding.

He did not respond.

And I'm okay with that—because my love for him doesn't need to change, even if it seems like his love for me has.

I deleted numbers from my phone—old coworkers who haven't responded to my texts or calls in months.

Freedom—from trying to make her like me.

I removed all social media from my phone, for now. I kept comparing myself to my husband's ex-girlfriends. Even though I blocked their profiles, I know myself. I'll start looking them up—or my ex-boyfriends, or someone new—and wonder:

What would life be like with someone
from my past or someone new?

Loving the same man and staying with one person has been my biggest growth—and the reward is worth it.

I've also decided to stop

Trying to get acceptance from my current bosses.

Because if I don't, I'll start people-pleasing, changing who I am, and eventually building a resentment. That doesn't mean I don't need to take direction. It just means I can act with kindness, even when I feel less than—or when I feel they're being unfair.

Have a blessed day.

Today I am grateful for:

- For surrender.
- That I don't know everything—and that I'm teachable.
- For getting out of my own way, in this moment. And sometimes, in *this moment i*s the best I've got.

Where are you still trying to prove your worth—and what would freedom look like if you stopped trying?

What are you grateful for today?

Still Employed. Still Loved. Still Growing.

I'm starting this Tuesday still employed. Not sure what each day will bring in that area of my life, but I'm still believing God's *got me.*

Today, I want to share about two beautiful friendships in my life.

One of my friends has been with me since *before* my addiction. She loved me through it—from a distance—but she *never* stopped loving me. She starts a new job today, and I'm so proud to call her my friend.

Another dear friend just moved into a new house this week. She met me when I was clean. Then she watched me relapse. And just like the first, she loved me from a distance—but never stopped loving me.

Both women have walked with me for years. They don't have the disease of addiction, but I think they understand it more than they'd probably like to. I'm sharing this today because I admire these two women deeply. I love them to the moon and back—and I couldn't ask for better friends.

Have a great day, my friend.

Today I'm grateful for:

- Friends who love al*l of* me, through every season.
- Staying in my marriage, even when leaving feels easier.
- The beautiful mess of a life God allows me to live today.

What are you grateful for today?

Five Years, One Marriage, and No More Packed Bags

Good morning, Friend,

I had a wonderful fifth wedding anniversary on Saturday. It's hard to believe we've made it this far—and I'm so thankful for the journey.

Seven years ago, I didn't think I wanted to be married. I also didn't want to be single, because I liked the chaos of a new relationship, especially with the type of men I dated. Once the chaos calmed down, I knew I'd move on to the next. The truth is, I never really had a plan to stick and stay in any romantic relationship. Who would have thought I could be in one relationship with one man, even when he doesn't always act the way I want him to?

Recovery has taught me that I am not a cheater. That was something I did, but it's not who I am. Because of God having so much grace, I no longer keep a bag packed in the trunk of my car *just in case* my marriage doesn't work out. (**That used to be my contingency plan.**)

I'm not here to tell you that marriage is easy or that I've fully recovered. I'm just sharing that when I put in the work and let God stay in the God seat, I start to get better.

Have an amazing day.

Today I am grateful for:

- My sponsor, who is not emotionally attached to my issues.
- My husband—who chooses to stay in the relationship with me. (It **takes two.**)
- A job that lets me go to the dentist without using a vacation day.

What old habits or backup plans have you laid down in order to stay and grow where you are?

What are you grateful for today?

Glue and German Chocolate Cake

For Mother's Day, my husband made me a German chocolate cake with coconut pecan icing—from scratch. He did it because my grandmother used to make me one every year for my birthday, and he wanted to make today special. Needless to say, it's already gone.

I spent the day at the zoo yesterday with four of my five children, two of my three grandbabies, and my husband. Later, I did the laundry, washed the dishes, swept the kitchen, made lunches for the next day, and got my clothes ready for work. Now, I'm finally sitting down to do my jigsaw puzzle.

You are the glue that holds the family together.

Today I am grateful for:

- To be a mom.
- To be a grandma.
- To be a woman.

What part of your role—mother, mentor, nurturer, or friend—are you most grateful for today?

What are you grateful for today?

Step Away from the Google

Last week, I visited the doctor for my annual physical and well-woman exam. I was so proud of myself—I was honest, and I didn't pass out during the bloodwork!

Later that day, my results came in. I messaged the doctor twice and called once, hoping someone would explain why some of my numbers were either too high or too low. The doctor kindly responded, letting me know she would follow up once *all* of my results were back. Still, I started obsessing over whether something was wrong with me.

If you ever find yourself in this situation, my suggestion is:
**Wait for the doctor to call you back—
and do not Google your results.**

But I didn't follow that advice. I decided I would figure it out myself. And now, after doing my research, I have even more fear. It's Tuesday night, and I still haven't heard back from the doctor.

Have a great evening.

Today I am grateful for:

- For the process of faith.
- That, even when I'm afraid to go to the doctor and get bloodwork, I do it anyway.
- That I'm no longer living in fear of my bloodwork results due to my past sexual behaviors, because I am in recovery now.

What's one area where you're trying to control the outcome—and how might surrender bring more peace than overthinking?

What are you grateful for today?

When Fear Looks Like Something Else

This week has been rough, and it's only Tuesday. Someone dear to me is not doing well health-wise. I've been angry about it and scared for them. I took my feelings out on my children's teacher yesterday, but I was able to make amends today.

Disappointed in my behavior.

Today, I found myself feeling less than and sad because I was looking for approval from others. After talking with a friend, I realized I was slipping backward in my recovery by seeking validation and comparing myself.

**Truth is, I have misplaced feelings—because
I'm sad over my dear person being sick.**

Here's some good news: my blood work came back. My vitamin D is low, and my blood sugar is almost too high. My doctor suggested I eat better and exercise.

My fear taught me that I don't always trust God.

Good night, sweet dreams, and sleep with the angels.

Today I am grateful for:

- For doctors who don't tell me to stop calling or messaging them, even when I'm spinning out of control.
- That God gives me opportunities to make amends to people who matter to me.
- For forgiveness—and for the chance to forgive those I thought I had already forgiven.

What fear might be hiding behind your frustration—and how can you respond with compassion instead of control?

What are you grateful for today?

When Surrender Hurts the Most

On Friday, a close family member showed signs of struggling with the disease of addiction. To numb the pain, I walked around a department store for hours, searching for a new outfit to change the way I *feel*.

I misplaced my emotions and started spiraling into thoughts about how I don't spend enough time with my mom or my kids. I judged every part of my life where I fell short of my expectations.

I quickly became angry with God. I fought so hard not to lose my children to the state during my active addiction, only to lose two close family members to addiction anyway. My fear now is whether they'll make it back to the rooms. I pray God keeps me clean so I can be ready and available… *if* they do make it back.

The hardest thing to do as a parent is to trust God with my children. As much as I love Him, you'd think that would be easy. Some days it is. Today, it's not.

I eventually realized what was going on—I'm hurting, and I'm hurting over my family member, and the fear of not knowing whether they'll ever return to recovery.

This is the space where trying *not* to be angry at God, and instead trusting that no matter what happens, it will be okay… feels almost impossible.

Later that evening, my husband went out to eat with his friends. I had the chance to go, but I chose to go home and walk through my feelings instead.

There was a time—not too long ago—when my husband could not go out to eat with a group that included women without me feeling insecure, without me making him feel bad for going. I see progress of recovery in my life.

My feelings did still get hurt this week when my GM went out to eat with the other managers and didn't invite me. I'm not sure what God is trying to teach me with this job, but I do know this: I didn't walk out. I didn't quit doing my work just because of how I felt. More progress.

Then on Monday, that same family member told me they had relapsed. They said they weren't sure if they were ready to be clean. They apologized for relapsing. I told them they didn't need to apologize to me because they didn't do this *to* me.

Thank you for walking with me.

Today I am grateful for:

- That I know the solution to all this pain is surrender.
- I don't have to walk through this alone, because I have *you to* walk with me.
- For life's lessons… even when I disagree with them.

Where are you trying to carry something that belongs in God's hands—and what would it look like to let it go, just for today?

What are you grateful for today?

The Dress Doesn't Define Me

I've been looking for a dress to wear to work at a department store for a few weeks now. I've bought three dresses, and I've taken two back. I'll probably either exchange the last one or return it, too. I have one of those bodies where my stomach is bigger than my chest. The feelings I used to carry about my body are starting to shift. Instead of searching for a pill, a surgery, a diet fad, or some slimming drink to fix how I feel, I'm learning to accept who I am—and I'm grateful for the body I have.

I'm grateful for the solution: *Keep taking the outfit back or stay in the store and try them on until one fits the way you like. Your body doesn't have to change—the outfit does.* And I'm grateful for accepting that my old boss hasn't called me back, not because she doesn't like me, but because she also has a life. I'm not her priority, and that's okay.

Have an amazing day. I love you!

Today, I'm also grateful for:

- Accepting something I used to feel ashamed of: I didn't go to school much growing up. My mom didn't make education a priority—her life was full of other things, and school just wasn't part of it. I never made it past elementary school, and for a long time, I carried that like a secret. But here's the truth: my education may not look like everyone else's, but that doesn't mean I'm less than. I've learned through living. I've grown through experience. I'm still a cool kid—because I'm being the most authentic version of me. I don't have to measure myself by someone else's ruler. I get to show up in the world with heart, honesty, and grit—and that counts for a lot.

- Today is my mother's 70th birthday. I'm also thankful that 22 years ago today, I buried my son—and this date, though heartbreaking, also marks the life of the woman who's walked beside me through every one of my mistakes: my mother.
- That I get to share all of this with you.

What's one part of your life you've tried to fix, when maybe what it really needed was acceptance?

What are you grateful for today?

Acceptance

It's been a week, and I'm still under the weather. Lately, I've been obsessing over getting a tummy tuck and a breast lift. I've talked about doing it for a while now, and recently, I've been researching prices and the expected recovery time.

I've ordered bathing suits and sent them back. I went to a department store and tried on several more, finally choosing one—not because I liked how it looked on me, but because I realized I don't like how *any* bathing suit looks on me. Because I don't like how *I* look.

My skin is sagging. My breasts don't perk up the way I want them to. I look in the mirror, and I don't like the person I see on the outside. I've lost over 50 pounds. I've dyed my hair, tattooed my lips and eyebrows, and keep my nails done most of the time. All of this—and I still struggle to feel good about myself.

I don't want the body I had at 20… truth is, I want a body I've never had. I think if I just get a makeover or surgery, I'll magically like myself more. I even got off social media to stop comparing myself and looking for reasons to believe my husband doesn't want me. Still, I don't feel enough. Logically, I know this is an inside job. But emotionally, it still feels as if I change the outside, the inside will follow.

I'm not saying I don't like myself at all, or that I'm completely unattractive. What I'm saying is that no matter how much I "improve" my appearance, something inside still feels empty.

Surrendering this to God is hard today. But I'm going to try. I'm going to let go of who I think I *should* look like and accept the way I look *right now.* Instead of putting unnecessary surgery on a credit card, I'll spend more time thinking about the things I do like about myself. And I'll ask God to help me see myself through *His* eyes, not mine.

Because if I take an honest look at what's going on… I know this isn't about my appearance. I'm hurting over the choices my adult children are making. I'm hurting over my older brother who is still not speaking to me. I'm afraid of losing my mom, who refuses to follow her doctors' advice. And I'm trying to fix all that pain by fixing the outside. But makeover or no makeover, life is still going to show up. No amount of beauty can protect me from my feelings.

Acceptance is my only true option.

Today, I'm grateful for:

- My husband, who told me I'm beautiful just the way I am—with my 45-year-old body—and that he loves me as I am.
- The opportunity to love myself. Hopefully through God's eyes, not just my own.
- Mini-wheat cereal.

Are you willing to trust that God's view of you is more important than your own—and let that shape how you see yourself?

What are you grateful for today?

Being Grateful

This past week, I've been on a roller coaster of emotions—and taking hostages along the way.

On Thursday, I felt well and wanted to attend a meeting, so I asked my husband to accompany me. But I had to stay home and wait for a package. I texted him and asked him to come home so I could take a bath. I told him it wasn't fair that he got to go out and I had to stay home and sign for the package. I hadn't agreed to be the one waiting—but someone had to be the adult, right?

I told myself not to keep texting him... yet I did it, anyway, knowing the pain it would cause both of us. I threw everything I could think of in his face over text. My husband didn't respond to my "book of messages"— he just gave me space and let me have my process.

Three days later, I was finally able to tell him the truth: I felt pretty that night, and I wanted to be out with him, sitting next to him. I was also hurting over not being able to stop the consequences of my loved ones' face in active addiction. If I had just led with honesty, I could've avoided so much damage.

Later, I took a quiz on love languages. My top love language is emotional connection, and my second is acts of service. Once my husband found out how to speak my love language, he bought books for us to read together on emotional intimacy. His actions showed me that he loves me, even on my worst days.

I also gained a more profound respect and understanding for the old-timers in the rooms. A friend shared with me how addiction still affects our predecessors in different ways. Getting older can bring loneliness, physical sickness, and painful thoughts like, "Why am I still feeling this way after all these years clean?" My friend reminded me that addiction doesn't care about age, race, or gender—we all struggle.

Recently, the owner of the company I work for asked if I'd be willing to take on another property and offered me a little more money. When I first got this job, I didn't like how my "gift" of employment was packaged. But God showed me today that what something appears to be may not be what it is. All things shiny are not good. What I once saw as "not good enough" is *exactly* what God has for me.

It's up to me to be grateful for what I have—and to start looking past my limited ideas of good or bad. I might just be surprised to find out I was wrong… and God is right.

Have a great day.

Today I am grateful for:

- The new opportunity to grow my career.
- My husband, his forgiveness, and his effort to make our marriage work.
- Kids' watermelon cough drop suckers—they're helping with my cough this week.

What might you be seeing as "not good enough" that could actually be a gift in disguise?

What are you grateful for today?

A Love Language I Didn't Know I Had

Good morning, my beautiful friend,

In the past couple of days, I've come to realize something new about myself: one of my love languages is *giving gifts*.

The gifts I give are intentional and personal, based on little things someone has shared with me over time. For example, if someone once told me they love yellow and Hershey's chocolate is their favorite, I'll surprise them with a yellow journal and a Hershey's bar, just because.

I don't do it for praise. I don't have any hidden motive. The truth is, I'm busy and don't always have the time I'd like to spend with everyone I care about. So, when I give a gift, it's my way of saying, "Hey, I'm thinking about you."

I didn't even fully realize this about myself until I said it out loud to another addict yesterday. And you know what? I like this part of me.

I spend so much time pointing out my flaws and the things I want to change. But today, I want to celebrate something I genuinely love about myself. And honestly, I like this part of me *a lot*.

Have a fantastic day, my beautiful friend.

Today I'm grateful for:

- Having friends!
- Liking something about myself!
- Having people I can text with both my struggles an*d my* wins!

What's one thing you genuinely *like* about yourself today?

What are you grateful for today?

Anger

This past week has been eye-opening. My mom had to stay overnight in the hospital. I had my husband text both of my brothers, because one of them has me blocked.

This makes me very angry.

As my mom was being admitted, all I could think about was being the only one of her three children handling everything—how my brothers were going to go on living their lives.

I became very resentful over something that never even happened.

My mom came home from the hospital. According to her, everything is fine. I spent most of my time in the ER lobby writing to God about how I wanted to act out, and how angry I've been.

**My sponsor suggested I seek outside help for
some of the things I'm going through.**

The irony is, I'm currently in Step Nine, believing I'm ready to make amends, with all this anger still inside me.

Still work to do.

I'm doing my best not to dress like I'm in my twenties or feel bad about getting older, even though it's been hard to accept. I'm trying to believe that it's all going to be okay.

I need God.

Have a thankful Tuesday.

Today I am grateful for:

- Distractions when I don't want to feel the pain.
- My sponsor and my support group.
- The people who walk with me through the pain, because it's too hard to bear alone.

What emotions are still living under the surface of your healing—and what would happen if you stopped pushing them down?

What are you grateful for today?

Old Patterns, New Truths

I was going to start this by attacking my husband's character—by telling you how wrong he is and how right I am. Instead, I'm going to keep it on me.

Not just this past week, but honestly, for the past six years, it seems like my husband has been trying to maintain friendships with women. And I've exhausted myself trying to control him, so much so that sometimes it feels easier to walk away than to be part of the solution.

The truth is, my problem with my husband having friendships with the opposite sex comes from *me*—my control, my jealousy, my insecurity. And I'm aware of it. So, it's time I do something different.

From 1997 to 2018—the better part of my life—I was consumed with learning how to attract and keep a man. I read books on what men like, how to tell if they're into me, how to become more desirable, and how to be a better lover. I studied men, manipulated them, and used my sexuality to get what I wanted. That became a big part of my identity.

I stopped reading those books when my husband and I officially committed to each other. But I didn't forget everything I learned.

To put it plainly: being "just friends" with a man, for me, feels like saying I can have just one drink and be fine. And I know where that thinking leads. That's my truth. But it doesn't mean my husband struggles with the same issues.

To me, friendship means sharing your heart—your likes and dislikes, what makes you laugh, what breaks you open. That kind of emotional intimacy is how I connect, regardless of gender. But when it comes to men, I haven't learned how to do that in recovery yet. I haven't figured out how to be friends with a man without stepping into old patterns.

And I think that's why I try to control my husband—because I'm scared. Scared he'll meet someone like the old me… and cheat.

I know how powerful sexuality can be. I once dated a man during my first clean stretch, and he refused to stop talking to women he'd slept with. One morning, we weren't even arguing—I just woke up and asked him to pack his things and leave. I never went back. I knew what I had to do to protect my peace.

So instead of being mad at my husband or walking away, I'm choosing to look at *myself* and trust God to work out the rest.

Have a fantastic week.

Today I am grateful for:

- That I'm no longer the woman I used to be.
- For the opportunity to stay in my marriage, even when my husband doesn't act the way I want him to.
- For all the female friendships I have today. Because of those women, I don't cheat, I don't run, and I don't blame, as often as I used to. I've learned to love myself because of the love you've shown me.

P.S. I've never told anyone about all the books I read about men—until today. How free do I want to be? *We do recover.*

What old beliefs or patterns are you finally ready to let go of?

What are you grateful for today?

The Power of the Pause

The past week was challenging for several reasons. My husband and I began the process of setting boundaries around having friends of the opposite sex. It's a practice, and so far, I'm still not okay with it. But I have let go of some of my control, at least in this moment.

My bonus son got into a physical fight with a child down the street. The other child hit him first, but it still wasn't okay for my son to hit back. There was a pause—neither one of them swung for a moment. That silence gave them both a chance to think. And even after that pause, they hit each other again.

I walked my son to the neighbor's house and had him apologize for his part and ask if there was anything he could do to make it right. On the way home, he asked if he could go to counseling because he felt bad for hitting the other child. I told him, "Of course. But if it's just because you hit someone back after they hit you, that's a normal human reaction. The part that will be harder to forgive is that you had time to think and still chose to hurt him again."

The very next day, I found myself thinking about a family member who had hurt me by calling me names, indirectly. He implied I was a loser for being in the rooms of recovery. My natural human reaction was to fire back—make him feel small, prove how great I am. I didn't hit him physically, but I struck him emotionally. And the most challenging part? I had time to think about it before I responded… and I did it anyway.

I didn't even stop to consider that maybe he was hurting too. Perhaps that was why he said what he did. A few moments later, I remembered the same lesson I had just tried to teach my son: *If you have time to think about your actions and still choose to cause harm, that's the part that will bother you the most.*

With my family member, I messed up the most by dismissing his feelings just because he's not an addict. As if being an addict somehow made me better than him. That stung to realize. But I also had to get honest about *why* his comment hurt me so much. It hurt because there's still a part of me that believes I shouldn't need recovery anymore, that I should be able to "just be a good person" without the program.

Do you see how sneaky my disease is?

It finds ways to make me feel ashamed of being an addict. And in doing that, I miss the lesson God is trying to teach me. My disease tells me the only way to get better is to stop being who I am.

But I know better today.

Have an awesome Tuesday.

Today I am grateful for:

- That I don't have to do recovery alone.
- To have a job that lets me leave early so I can watch my son play football on Tuesday nights.
- That—even if I never write that book I've dreamed about since my teens—I still get to show up, share who I am, and let you in on both my struggles and my wins.

What have you said or done in a moment of pause that you wish you hadn't—and what can that moment still teach you today?

What are you grateful for today?

Reconnecting on a Wednesday

Good morning, my friend,

I put everything before texting you yesterday, *Tuesday's Perspective*, because I want to ensure that my job is satisfied with my performance. The truth is that staying connected to you is important to me. I am working on avoiding gossip and staying away from those who gossip. Yesterday, I did not do this very well. Today, I want to lift people up and point out what I like about them.

I am grateful to you. Have a great day.

Today I appreciate you for:

- How thoughtful you are
- Making your family a priority
- How you never discuss anyone

Who do you need to reconnect with today—and how can you choose encouragement over judgment?

What are you grateful for today?

Learning to Love
Without Conditions

Good morning, Friend,

Today is already a good day, because I'm grateful for my nephew, who turns eight today, and I get to be a part of his life.

There are so many things to be thankful for. Even when I don't understand why God does things the way He does, I trust that He has my back. And even though I've struggled with addiction and self-righteousness for much of my life, I can see now that God loves me anyway.

Recently, a couple of friends chose not to continue our friendship.

At first, I felt hurt.

Then I got angry.

But now, after some time to process and sit in acceptance, I've been able to ask God to show me where *I* might be loving people conditionally, so I can learn to treat others the way I want to be treated:

With *unconditional love.*

Today I am grateful for:

- My nephew's joyful spirit.
- The space to reflect instead of react.
- A God who never gives up on me.

Where in your life are you still loving with conditions—and how can you shift toward grace?

What are you grateful for today?

A New Kind of Freedom

I'm at work today because I took yesterday off. My second-to-youngest son has been sick for a couple of days now, so all our 4th of July plans had to be canceled. Even so, I'm incredibly grateful. I'm grateful for a husband who steps in without hesitation, even though my son is not his biological son.

My husband had made plans to go to a pool party today and spend time with our kids until I got off work. But he never once complained that those plans had to change. In fact, when I brought it up this morning, his response was:

**"Go to work. Don't worry. Our son—I'll take care of him.
And don't stress about the plans changing.
This is life happening, and I wouldn't want to be anywhere else."**

My first thought was, *Wow.* What did I do to deserve a man who puts us first?

What a beautiful day to celebrate *freedom*, not just in this country, but freedom from the disease of addiction. What a day to be thankful for.

I love you, my beautiful friend.

Today I am grateful for:

- A husband who chooses love in action.
- The freedom to be present, even when plans change.
- Recovery that gives me peace in the unexpected.

What does true freedom look like in your life today?

What are you grateful for today?

God's Got Me—And That's Enough

The people at my job are starting to like me… or maybe *I'm* starting to enjoy *it*. It's not exactly my idea of "fancy," but the people who work there genuinely care about each other.
Money should never replace genuine people.

I've started another weight loss journey.
This time, it's more for my health than my looks.

Let's see if I follow through. I need to remember that God is much more powerful—and consistently so—than I am.
God's got me.

I learned something new over this past weekend:
I have friends who want me around.

I can stop looking over the fence, fantasizing about what my life would be like if I were *them*.

Have a great day, my friend.

Today I'm grateful for:

- For the blessings I have—and that I no longer want to trade them for anyone else's.
- My husband got up with me last night and took care of me while I was feeling sick.
- For a couple of new relationships that might turn into friendships. **(No forcing. No controlling the outcome. Just letting them grow if they're meant to.)**

What's one area of your life you can choose to enjoy today—just as it is?

What are you grateful for today?

The Growth Only God and I Can See

I had my 90-day review at my new job, and it went well. The owner listened to me and gave thoughtful feedback on areas I could improve. I wasn't defensive, accusatory, or looking to blame anyone for my mistakes. I took responsibility and stayed positive.

I am not just a warm body filling a spot.

I started my weekend off by telling my middle daughter how to live her life, *based on my standards.* Once I realized I was crossing boundaries, I apologized—without making a judgmental comment.

I do not get a vote in my grown-up children's lives.

Our female neighbor has been texting my husband for help with different things. She's younger than me and has a husband of her own. I asked my husband why she wasn't asking *him* for help. I started to feel angry. Then I remembered—I don't have control over my husband. We talked about my concern, and I let it go.

My husband has to decide what's appropriate in our marriage without me correcting him like one of our children.

My daughter let my husband and me throw a birthday party for our grandkids this past Saturday.

This time last year, she wouldn't even speak to me.

Have a wonderful day!

Today I am grateful for:

- Learning to let go of control—even if I have to do it over and over again.
- All the noise in my house from having family and friends gathered.
- Having a home to clean up after hosting an event.

Where have you seen progress in yourself—quiet, slow growth that maybe only you and God could measure?

What are you grateful for today?

The "F*It" Button

Being married—sometimes—is one of the hardest things to do. It can feel so much easier just to hit the "f*** it" button than to actually work through the issues.

One of my predecessors once told me, "Imagine what your life would be like if you and your husband weren't together." I sat with that wisdom for a moment.

Lately, things in my marriage have been tough to walk through. That same voice of wisdom echoed again: **"Be grateful for your husband. Imagine if you were alone."**

I *love* my husband. And I also understand the pain I would cause—both to my family and to myself—if I gave up just because I felt like I was right.

Have a great day, friend.

Today I am grateful for:

- That I don't have to be *right*, even when my anger feels justified by what someone else did.
- For a God who gives me the strength to walk through the hard stuff instead of running from it.
- For my life—and I remember that my husband and I are both human, both still a work in progress.

When you're tempted to walk away, what wisdom can you pause and sit with instead?

What are you grateful for today?

The Truth, the Fears, and the Pattern

Part One

A few days ago, I shared in a meeting—right in front of my husband—that I was struggling to stay married. And I did it intending to hurt his feelings. A few days later, he told me how much it hurt him when I talked about leaving. The truth is, I was hurt by something he said before that meeting… and I wanted to hurt him back.

This kind of behavior hurts *me*, too.

That tit-for-tat stuff that used to work for me in early recovery? It doesn't work anymore.

Part Two

I also learned something new about myself this week: I've been afraid that once my husband finishes working all of his steps, he won't want to be with me anymore. Deep down, I've probably been trying to leave him *before* he has a chance to leave *me*.

But the truth is—I love my husband.

And starting today, I won't say in a meeting that I want to leave him because it's not true.

Work

This week, the owner of my company backed out of a deal he asked me to put together for a client *I* prospected. Then, after pulling out, he went back to the client saying he wanted to move forward again—but by then the client had lost interest.

I was embarrassed. I was upset with how it was handled and disappointed about losing the client. However, here's the truth: My boss has the right to run his company as he sees fit.

Money

Every weekend for a while now, I've been spending money to change how I feel. And I'm paying for it. This is the fourth—or maybe even fifth—time I've run up my credit cards. Then I stress about how I'm going to pay them off.

Same pattern. Exact question: *How did I get here again?*

Have a great evening.

Today I am grateful for:

- That I don't have to act on the thought of getting divorced.
- That I'm not the one running four hotels and having to make company-wide decisions.
- My kids go back to school tomorrow—these teachers can take their kids back! (Just kidding.) But really, I'm grateful to be present and to be an active parent in al*l of* their lives.

What's one part of your life you've tried to fix, when maybe what it really needed was a new pattern?

What are you grateful for today?

Forgiveness

Thirteen years ago, someone I loved hurt my family; people I love deeply. I was faced with the reality of going to trial to put that person in prison for a long time.

A week before the trial date, the District Attorney called and asked what I wanted to happen. He told me I had two options:

1. Put this person on extensive probation, where they could also be offered help
2. Take it to trial, where they could receive 10 years to life

My response was, "I'm not the judge over this person. I want to go with whatever the justice system sees fit for that type of crime." Then—and this part was big for me—I forgave them. I released them to God.

Every once in a while, I still think of that person and what they did, and I feel the anger rise again. But God gently nudges me and reminds me: **You've already forgiven them.**

This past week, I had the opportunity to help someone I used to be extremely jealous of, as I feared my husband would return to her. But instead of clinging to that old jealousy, I leaned into willingness. I helped where I could.

I had to forgive *myself* for the pain I caused in my marriage over a fantasy I created… the one where I wasn't good enough.

Because of God and the recovery journey He's walking me through, I'm starting to let go of that lie.

Today is my oldest son's 24th birthday. And he's doing exactly what I was doing at that age. Sometimes I time-travel back to the version of me who was parenting back then—and I blame myself for the choices my grown kids make now. But then I pause, and I remind myself:

"Oh yeah—I've already forgiven *that,* Jennifer."

Today I am grateful for:

- The courage to choose forgiveness over resentment
- God's gentle reminders that I am not who I once was
- A new perspective on old pain—one filled with grace

What area of your life are you still holding onto, even after forgiveness has been spoken?

What are you grateful for today?

Not Getting a Raise

Children (Grownups)

My husband is planning to turn off our grown children's phones if they don't pay their bills by the first of the month. At first, I was mad—I didn't want anything to happen to them. But the truth is, they're adults. It's not my or my husband's responsibility to keep paying their bills.

Children (at Home)

I'm enjoying every moment with them… except when I'm brave enough to go upstairs and see the mess they've made. Even then, I'm still grateful.

Husband

He's doing what he needs to do for our family. We don't always get along, and I still don't wholly agree with turning off the phones. But at the end of the day, my husband and I are a team. We *have* to be united—because if we're not, our children will manipulate the situation. Another recovering addict helped me see that yesterday.

Work

They're still not giving me a raise—and won't say why. I was told it would happen in the third quarter, and now the third quarter ends this week. My current boss told me to stay open-minded and not shut down opportunities elsewhere. I took that as a sign to start applying, so I obsessively did that yesterday.

Today, I'm asking God to *bless it or block it* when it comes to finding a new job. The thing is, I'm happy where I am. I want to grow within the company, but I've heard they might be selling the hotels. We'll see what happens.

Friends

I don't stay in contact with every friend every day, but I'm *so* grateful for the ones who've stuck around. And I'm done feeling sorry for myself about the two women who don't want anything to do with me. Their absence doesn't erase the love I've received from others.

Older Brother

His opinion doesn't matter. Another addict helped me with that truth. It doesn't matter if he doesn't want to talk to me or thinks I'm a loser. What matters is what *I* think of me.

Half the time, I think I'm pretty great. The other half, not so much. It's a constant balance—but my brother doesn't define me.

Recovery

I get to process *Tradition Seven* in the IP *The Triangle of Self-Obsession* on Friday. More will be revealed.

Have a blessed day, my friend.

Today I am grateful for:

- For the ability to hear.
- That I can type notes in my phone.
- For a God who allows me to come to Him with whatever is on my mind and heart.

How can you trust God with your future—job, family, and relationships—without trying to control the outcome?

What are you grateful for today?

Changing My Behavior

Gossiping

This past week, I was talking with another addict about someone else's behavior, and before I caught myself, I started gossiping. Once I realized the conversation was unproductive and harmful, I made amends for my part in it. But I also noticed how, because of what I heard, I began to view the person we were talking about in a negative light.

Awareness

After the conversation ended, I became aware of how often I cast my husband, children, mom, and others in a negative light when I share certain things in group settings or with multiple people. I now understand why it's so important to have a sponsor and a trusted support group—otherwise, I risk character-assassinating the very people I love the most.

Amends

I want to make amends to you for the way I've spoken about my husband and family members—and even about myself. If you ever catch me doing it again, please don't hesitate to call me out.

Having a Husband

At a meeting, I was venting to a friend about how my husband frustrates me. She lovingly and quietly said, "Having your husband is a blessing." Her words meant so much, especially since she lost her husband unexpectedly. That moment brought my self-righteousness down a few notches.

Patterns

Once a month, my body throws a party without my permission, and my emotions spiral. During that time, I can quickly paint myself as a victim instead of taking responsibility for my own life and behavior.

Have an amazing day, my beautiful friend. If no one has told you today, you are loved.

Today I am grateful for:

- The chance to practice not character-assassinating people who hurt my feelings.
- The five women in my support group—especially my sponsor—with whom I can share everything.
- The discipline of writing a Step 10 every day for 31 days. It's teaching me that I'm neither perfect nor always right—and that it's okay, and often good, to be wrong. It's time to take responsibility, ask my Higher Power for forgiveness, and forgive myself.

What story do you tell about someone you love that might be shading how you see them?

What are you grateful for today?

My Feelings Are Real

This past week has been one of the hardest since I got clean.

I stopped taking my antidepressants—under my doctor's care—completely this week. There were moments I couldn't stop sobbing out loud. Knowing my kids might hear me, I decided to explain—at least a little—so they wouldn't worry too much.

I've spent the last two nights crying—long, hard, cries—mainly on the floor of my closet. The first night, my husband tried to comfort me. By the second night, I realized just how much I've been leaning on him emotionally. Too much.

The reason I stopped my medication. My libido has been nearly nonexistent, and it's caused tension in my marriage, especially in our sex life. My husband and I talked it through, and we agreed to try a break from the meds. We both said if things got too hard, I'd go back on them.

Well, things have gotten harder than I expected. So much so that last night, my husband slept upstairs.

He's now asked me to start retaking my medication. And here's the part that might not make sense to some, especially knowing how fragile things feel between us, how close our marriage feels to unraveling:

I don't want to go back on the meds.

Not just yet.

Because of these feelings? They're *real*. And I want to feel all of them.

I don't want to keep running from my pain. I've done that for too long. I don't like quitting just because life gets hard. I *do* understand why my husband is frustrated—*I'm* frustrated with myself too. I've depended on him for too long to keep me emotionally okay.

My hope? That he can hold on with me through this and walk with me to the other side.

Now, I'm not dismissing his behavior—because honestly, it hasn't helped the process much. Or maybe… it has? The truth is, with him emotionally unavailable, I've finally been forced to call on my God. It's either that or sit in the pain alone.

All this time, I've asked my husband to carry a weight only God was meant to hold.

That first night I broke down, it reminded me of the last time I cried like that—New Year's Eve, 2015. I was alone in my home, just God and me, when I laid the drugs down.

I woke up on January 1st, 2016, and I haven't picked up a drug, a drink, or a cigarette since.

I'll be honest—yesterday, I thought about using again. Not necessarily substances—but people, places, things—*anything* to numb the pain of feeling like my husband wants nothing to do with me. But God stepped in. I went to a meeting instead.

That decision was a big deal. Because in the past, I would've stayed home, tried to fix things right then, and skipped the meeting.

Yes, my husband said some hurtful things. But so did I. Maybe he was speaking from anger and pain, just like I was. That doesn't make the words hurt less. But it *does* help me have empathy. It helps me *recognize* the pain.

I almost didn't send this week's perspective. It exposes a lot—my marriage, my mistakes, my husband's struggles, too. I realized I *need* to share the hard stuff. Because someone else might need to know:

We're still walking through it.

And so far, neither of us has left.

Have a blessed day, my friend.

I love you.

Today I'm grateful for:

- My husband, even though it hurts right now.
- These emotions I get to fe*el,* because I've medicated them for the last seven years.

- The way my God loves me. Sometimes, it just takes a while for me to see the pain as a blessing.

When was the last time you chose to feel something hard instead of running from it?

What are you grateful for today?

Not Feeling Well and Still Feeling Grateful

Today, I'm not feeling well—my throat is sore and feels swollen. But I'm thankful for the awareness of feeling sick, because there was a time I wouldn't even notice. I used to numb everything—sickness, sadness, pain—with whatever I could find outside of myself. I didn't care.

Today, I can feel discomfort and respond with self-care. I'm resting. I'm taking cold medicine as prescribed. And I'm letting my body heal.

Last night, I kept waking up coughing. I didn't want to disturb my husband, so I grabbed my pillow and headed for the couch. But he saw me and said, *"No, baby. Stay here with me. I'm so sorry you're feeling bad. Let me hold you."* He held me, and this morning, he got up early, without complaint, and went to work.

I live a good life today.

Thank you for listening. Have a great day.

Today I am grateful for:

- For the ability to feel sick, because that means I'm not high.
- That my husband cares about how I feel.
- For that magical day-and-night cold medicine set.

How can you choose gratitude even in moments when you feel weak or uncomfortable?

What are you grateful for today?

Surrender Meets Stress

I've started a new practice over the last couple of days: no TV after 9 p.m. Instead, I read a book until 9:30. It takes practice—because honestly, I still *want* to watch TV. I notice that desire gets stronger when I'm emotionally overwhelmed, especially when it comes to my adult children and everything they're going through.

There's a sadness in my heart this morning. My daughter came over at 1:45 a.m. because she was afraid of the wind and worried about the safety of her children. I didn't respond. That decision has been weighing on me. It *should* have been easy, but when you're married and share a home, every decision you make impacts someone else. My choices also affect my husband.

I'm trying to stay focused on work today. I had a Teams call with my boss last week about my performance. This is the job I wanted, but lately I've felt like I jumped into something way over my head.

This—this is where surrender meets stress. And where I remind myself: I don't need to carry it all. God's got me.

Have a great day!

Today I'm grateful for:

- A home that keeps the wind out.
- A job that stretches and challenges me.
- Substitute sugar with zero calories, so I can still enjoy my coffee. Because let's be real, black coffee with no*thing in* it is gross.

What's something you've been holding onto that you can surrender to God today?

What are you grateful for today?

The Present of Being Present

Me:

This Christmas season, I've been in a joyfully giving mood. I danced in the kitchen to Christmas music while cooking pork chops. I watched a Christmas movie all by myself, and I was completely okay with it. I also watched *a movie* with my family.

Friendships:

I went to a Christmas party and, for the first time in forever, I felt like myself, without any drugs or alcohol in my system. This year, I can even say: without antidepressants. I felt comfortable in my own skin. I didn't try to make the most popular people in the room like me by changing who I am, only to get upset later when they didn't respond to my manipulation the way I wanted them to. I was *present in the present.* And it turns out—I have friends, just being me.

Children:

I've eased up on trying to make my children do everything the way I think it should be done. I'm learning to be thankful they're doing it at all. I told my daughter I couldn't watch her kids because I had plans, and that was hard. I know she's trying to work and take care of her children. I'm still working on boundaries—and not being too rigid with them.

Husband / Marriage:

My husband shared some hard-to-hear news with me, and I didn't react in a way that made him feel like he had to pretend to be perfect. What he shared hurt, but I'm so grateful he felt safe enough to be honest and be himself. I certainly haven't made this easy for him—or for the people closest to me.

Validation:

I sent a video and a picture of my puppy to my old bosses. Right after I sent them, I got that pit-in-the-stomach feeling and knew it had been a mistake. I'm having a hard time letting go of that chapter in my life and building new relationships with the people I work with now. I'm a good employee. I don't need others to confirm that—I need to believe it myself.

Have a magnificent day!

Today I am grateful for:
- The sound of Christmas music, because I used to get annoyed when I heard it. Now I'm just thankful I ca*n h*ear.
- My husband and family—not because they're perfect, but because they're not. That takes the pressure off all of us.
- The taste of boba and brown sugar tea with cream.

How can you continue to embrace the present moment without letting old patterns and relationships pull you backward?

What are you grateful for today?

The Gift of the Christmas Spirit

Over the past seven days, there's been so much to be thankful for.

Higher Power

My beliefs about this holiday vary, but I believe in—and love—Yahweh, the God who was born and died for me.

While I don't know if Christmas marks the actual earthly birth of Jesus, the Son of my God, I do know this: I celebrate because God loves me. And today, I'm clean.

If you know me, you know I don't agree with everything a preacher says—or with every interpretation of the Bible. But I believe my purpose is to love God and love others to the best of my ability… and to trust God with the rest.

Work

This year, we had two Christmas parties—one at each of the properties I manage. I couldn't make it to the third one, but my GM at one location gave me the perfect gifts: a mini flat iron and a gift card for my favorite lunch spot during the workweek.

When I reflect on my past jobs, I'm especially grateful for where I am now. The last place I worked was difficult. The one before that wouldn't even consider giving me a raise, without explanation.

Here? Even when things don't go my way, I have hope. I believe I can persevere and continue to grow.

Family

Tonight, my children are coming over to celebrate Christmas Eve.

We've even invited my bonus son's mom to join us.

A year ago, this would've felt impossible. The idea of my husband's ex setting foot in our home? Not a chance.

However, back then, my insecurities and low self-worth dictated my reactions.

Today, I'm more confident and grounded in God's love for me. I'm no longer seeking validation from men—or money. Just for today, I'm at peace with who I am.

Remembering Loved Ones

This season, I've been thinking a lot about the graves I haven't visited lately—my son, my grandparents, my father, my cousin, and friends like Chase and Niecy.

Tomorrow evening, I'm planning to host a candlelight vigil at home in their honor. Instead of focusing on the pain of loss, I want to remember the joy they brought into my life.

Even with all the chaos, the holidays gave me some of the best memories I've ever had.

Christmas Reflections

I've heard many people say the holidays are hard, and I used to feel that way, too. But this year, I've let go of some burdens. (Even if God had to pry them out of my hands.)

I'm learning it's okay to feel whatever I feel. Sadness, happiness, and everything in between—those emotions are blessings. They remind me that I'm alive. That I'm present.
I don't run from my feelings anymore. I don't numb them with drugs, alcohol, or toxic relationships.

Recovery has given me the ability to experience life, just as it is.

Merry Christmas Eve and Happy New Year! I'm grateful to you, my friend.

Today I am grateful for:

- Christmas lights and the spirit of celebration. No matter who created the holiday or how it evolved, it's a time to feel joy.

- Stepping away from social media while I work through this round of [Al-Anon's Twelve] Steps and Traditions. It's freeing not to seek validation or vent online.
- Small joys—like wearing a shirt that says, *"Santa, define naughty." I* may not believe in Santa… but I believe in the Christmas spirit and living my best life.

What blessings are you holding onto, and which burdens is God asking you to release?

What are you grateful for today?

A Love I Never Expected

Good morning, Friend,

Today, I had the privilege of attending my bonus son's 4th grade graduation. I'm so grateful for moments like this—when I get to be *present*.

My heart melted as I watched him scan the crowd, looking for me. And when he finally spotted me, he smiled and waved. The parents clapped as all the kids walked through the hall, proud and excited.

After the ceremony, he rushed over and gave me a couple of hugs, telling me he loved me. I almost started crying. Because honestly, I never thought I could love someone else's children the way I love my own.

Moments like this show me just how important it is to be there for all five of our kids, as often as I can. And some days, I wonder…

What did I do to deserve all the love I receive from these beautiful children?

Today I am grateful for:

- Bonus children who feel like mine.
- The chance to witness milestones, big and small.
- A heart that keeps learning how to love more deeply.

What old patterns are you ready to release so you can grow in your relationships?

What are you grateful for today?

Reflecting Back on Last Year

Recovery

I stayed clean for another full year, by the grace of God and my willingness to cooperate and pray for help. Some days were better than others, and the only thing I've done perfectly in recovery is *stay clean*. That hasn't come without pain, lessons, surrender, and a deeper willingness to change.

Work

As I look back on last year, I realize the job I have now is the one I prayed for. My hope is that I keep showing up, learning, and doing the best I can every day. I ask God to help me keep this job and be a good employee. Most days, I work hard—I show up early and stay late when I can, without taking from my family.

I was really hurt by how I was treated at my last job. And the one before that—I had built some great relationships, but when I left, those people stopped talking to me. I have to own my part in that. When they stopped speaking to me, I reacted by trying to take some of their business. I also blamed them without recognizing how immaturely I was handling things.

I'm learning to let go, forgive myself and others, and move forward.

Marriage

My relationship with my husband has been one of the hardest to navigate. There were a couple of times this year when I didn't know if I would stay—or if I even wanted to. But I knew I didn't want to put another man, or drugs, or alcohol, on top of my feelings just to escape them.

Now shopping—that's another story. I go to thrift stores, so I justify it by saying it doesn't cost much. But let me tell you: when I run from my feelings, it doesn't matter *what* I use—the cost is always high. I've learned that if I stop and ask God for help *before* I reach for the credit card, I save myself a lot of pain.

Last year, I also learned that I don't have to tell my husband how to live his life or try to control his behavior, so I don't get hurt. I can share my boundaries, speak up about what bothers me, and let go of the outcome. It's not up to me how he behaves—or how he reacts.

I love my husband. He is a good man. Staying married is something I have to ask God to help me with too. When I prayed for a husband and God gave me one, I also needed to pray about how to *keep* him—and how to stay.

Children

I've learned to let my adult children live their lives however they choose. They're grown. They don't need my advice or commentary. I no longer get a vote. I also don't need to keep myself locked in guilt over the past, replaying all the mistakes I made or what I could've done differently. I must trust that the same God who watches over me will watch over them too.

Now, about the children still living at home... Remember how I shared that my last job hurt my feelings? Well, I started behaving the same way with my kids—critical, short-tempered—and God graciously showed me how that felt so I could make it right.

I still ask God to help me not yell or constantly point out what they're doing wrong. Instead, I'm learning to point out what they're doing *right*. That works in my marriage too.

This past week, my boys lost our new puppy. They forgot about her in the backyard, and she slipped through a small opening in the fence. I was so angry—I grounded them on the spot. But after I calmed down, my husband gently reminded me: we *all* had a part in losing the puppy. I rushed home from work and found her next door. When she heard my voice, she started crying. My heart overflowed when I held her again.

On the car ride home, I had been saying things like, *"Those effing kids are so irresponsible."* Even though no one heard me, I was convicted in my heart. I gathered my boys, hugged them, told them they weren't grounded, and that we would all learn together how to better care for the puppy. We all had a responsibility.

The next few days, I kept asking God to forgive me for what I said—because I love my kids deeply. I remembered when I couldn't see them or spend time with them because of CPS.

Today, I have full custody of my children—and my husband's children. God reminded me that I once asked for my kids back, and He gave them to me. Now, just like I do with my job and my marriage, I have to ask God how to *keep* them and how to continue restoring our relationships.

Friends

Today, I have female friends—something I never thought possible. I used to not like women. I didn't trust them. But that's because I didn't like or trust *myself.* I've worked hard in this area of my life. I have friends now who *want* to spend time with me—intentionally.

I kept asking God for friends all throughout last year. And what I learned is that everything I wanted in a friend, I needed to become. Then I would start attracting those people. And it's true. My life is now surrounded by beautiful friendships—women who would walk through anything with me, because I would do the same for them. Just like with every other relationship I've mentioned—when I ask God for more, I also ask Him how to *keep* it.

Family

I've learned to accept my family members for who they are and where they are. God didn't just help me accept them—He also helped me love them. I invite them to Thanksgiving and Christmas dinners without expecting them to act a certain way. I've learned not to judge them afterward or compare my life to theirs. The same way I want acceptance from others—I need to be willing to give it.

Health

I had a bit of a health scare this year. For a moment, they thought I might have cancer. So far, every scan and test has come back clear. And I am *so* grateful.

I live a life today that I didn't earn and don't deserve. An old sponsor once asked me, when I was trying to get clean: *"Do you choose to be chosen?"* I didn't understand what that meant then. But I do now.

To me, it means God *chose* me—to walk into the rooms, to get clean, and to stay clean. And I get to choose, every day, whether I'll live the life He gave me—or whether I'll run because of fear or feelings.

My hope for you, my friend, is that each new year brings you:
- Blessings
- Honest feelings
- Real joy
- A little pain to keep you growing
- Lots of gratitude
- And full acceptance

I love you. Have an amazing year.

Today I am grateful for:

- A new year filled with fresh beginnings.
- The lessons of last year—both painful and beautiful.
- God's grace that carried me through another year clean.

As you step into the new year, how can you carry forward the lessons of surrender, humility, and gratitude into the year ahead?

What are you grateful for today?

A Bag on the Ground

Good morning, Friend,

A few minutes ago, I stopped at the gas station to get gas and a drink. As I walked past the pump, I noticed a small baggie on the ground with some substance inside. I was shocked to see it, especially in this stage of my recovery.

While I was picking out a drink, a police officer walked in, grabbed something to drink, and said, "Have a nice day." A few moments later, I saw him again at the front of the store. He smiled and told me once more to have a good day.

As I turned to leave, a woman came out of the restroom. She looked like she might be struggling—maybe even using. When I walked back to my car, I saw that same little baggie still lying on the ground. And in that moment, it hit me how truly blessed I am. I got to talk to an officer today—not in fear, not hiding, but just being present and kind. I wasn't the woman in the store, making no sense, lost in addiction.

With everything going on in my life, I'm not going to pretend I haven't *thought* about using. But I can tell you with confidence, my life today is so much better than whatever was in that little bag.

I love God. I love my life. And today, I feel so loved by Him, because He took the time to show me what my life looks like *without* using.

Have a great day. God loves you, and so do I.

Today I am grateful for:

- The gift of sobriety and freedom from addiction.
- Encounters that remind me of God's protection and grace.
- Being present in my life without fear or shame.

What reminders has God placed in your path to show you how far you have come?

What are you grateful for today?

Support

❧

Husband

When I tell you I have a good man, it's because I get a front-row seat to his life.

My husband coaches our son's basketball team. On Saturday, they had their first game, and they were winning by a lot. I watched as my husband called a timeout. When the boys came back on the court, I noticed they weren't playing as hard. They weren't taking as many shots. And then the other team started putting points on the board.

That's when I realized—my husband had asked his team to ease up and let the other team get a few shots in. True humility is knowing you're good at something and still looking out for the interests of others. Just because you *can* doesn't mean you *should*.

Could Have Been Me

As I sat at dinner, I watched a man get pulled over and given a sobriety test through the window. Then, I saw the officers put him in the back of the patrol car and tow his vehicle away.

There was a time when that would've irritated me. I used to think, *"Why can't the cops just let people live their lives and leave people alone?"*

But today, I felt gratitude. That man being arrested may have saved lives, including his own. That could have been me.

Support

Today, I celebrated 9 years clean with my home group and friends in my support network.

Who would've thought God would take a cheater like me and make me into a woman that other women trust to talk to about their marriages?

Who would've thought the kind of mom I used to be would become the mom—and present grandma—I am today?

Who would've thought a girl who didn't go to school and had no formal education would one day become a writer, sending out *Tuesday's Perspective* to people who *want* to read what she writes?

Who would've thought that girl would become this woman, one day at a time, through the rooms of recovery and God?

I used to think I had no friends, and that no one liked me. Today, I *have* friends. And people *do* like me. Thank you for being part of my recovery.

Today I am grateful for:

- Recovery and for having 9 years clean
- The women who trust me to show up and be available
- God—and for how He uses *you to* make me a better me

How can you recognize God's hand in the places where He's transformed you —and trust Him to keep writing your story?

What are you grateful for today?

Overlooking Miracles, Las Vegas

I went on a work trip with my husband to Las Vegas. Neither of us had ever been, and my job was gracious enough to let me work remotely, 19 hours away from home. Even though I was limited in what I could get done, I still worked.

My whole perspective on work has changed. I've always been a bit of a workaholic, but my motives now are completely different. Today, I work hard to be dependable and to live with integrity, not to escape or prove something, but because I want to do what's right.

There was a time when I used to work to avoid being a mom, because I didn't think I was good at it. I also used to work as many hours as possible to support my addictions—whether it was drugs, men, money, shopping, or buying things I couldn't afford for my kids, to make up for my guilt.

While we were in Vegas, one of our children was going through something, and I let it affect my mood and how I treated my husband. I'm currently praying that God guides us and our children through *His* will, not Jennifer's.

Now, back to the Vegas trip. My husband and I walked the Strip and Fremont Street. We saw men and women dressed… lightly. I'll admit, seeing those women with what looked like "perfect" bodies made me feel a little insecure—but only for a moment.

My best defense against such thoughts is gratitude. I thank God for what I *do* have. The best part of our trip? My husband and I made a budget and stuck to it. We even came home having spent less than we planned. That, to me, is a *miracle.* We've both had toxic patterns with money in the past, and we've argued over finances before. But this time? No fights. Just teamwork.

Have a wonderful day, my friend.

Today I am grateful for:

- My job that allows me to take trips with my husband, even without vacation time.
- A husband who wanted to experience Vegas to*gether f*or the first time.
- The body I have and the ability to walk.

How often do you overlook everyday miracles because you're too focused on your insecurities or frustrations?

What are you grateful for today?

Here's What's Been Going On

Let me start by saying: being a parent is one of the most rewarding, heartbreaking, challenging, and joy-filled experiences in my life.

Lately, I've been watching patterns and behaviors in my children that mirror my own past. It takes a lot of prayer, patience, and empathy to allow them to be precisely where they are. And it takes *even more* prayer to trust God to take care of them. Even though I *know* God is capable—and far more powerful than I'll ever be—there's still a part of me that wants to step in and say: *"I'm the mom. And I disagree with how You're handling this, God. Let me help You!"*

That's when God gently reminds me: *"Kiddo, I took care of you when you didn't even care about yourself. Your mom felt the same way about you—and look, you're still okay, aren't you?"*

Vegas Trip

My husband and I went to Vegas together for the first time. Let me just say—it's *not* like the movie *Casino.* There were so many women with amazing bodies getting paid just for how they look, and I'll admit—it didn't help with my obsession over wanting bigger boobs or a tummy tuck. However, I then had to stop and practice gratitude. Because when I used to get paid for the way I looked, and I took that money, it ended up costing me the *most.*

Body Image & Social Media

Lately, God has been helping me abstain from social media while I follow through on the commitments I've made. I've still been taking pictures, but without filters. I'm learning to accept myself exactly as I am.

Over the weekend, I got really sick. The pictures I took showed it—dark circles under my eyes, wrinkles on my face. And you know what? I'm grateful to see the *real* me, for better or worse. I still haven't had my nails or toes done. Acceptance is key.

I'm turning 46 on the 17th of this month, and I *might* glam myself up again… maybe. There's been a new kind of freedom in accepting how I look without all the enhancements. Don't get me wrong, I still enjoy them! But I'm not depending on them to define my worth.

I love myself today. And just so you know, I love you too.

Today I am grateful for:

- Getting paid for the work I do today.
- Learning how to love myself, for who I am and what I look like.
- The process, the progress, the growing pains, and the deepening relationship I have with myself.

Are you willing to trust God's care for your children and yourself more than your own need to control?

What are you grateful for today?

Being Grateful for What I Have

I've been on this search to fill a void instead of letting God fill it. I've been asked, *"Have you gone to God with your request?"* Most of the time, my answer is yes.

I've been at my job for over a year now and not once have any of my three locations hit their bonuses. It's been discouraging, to say the least. I've received several calls and emails about how my staff treats both guests and one another. The funny part is, I *believed* God gave me this job. So, I'm trying to stick it out for at least three years. Why three years? Because I've never stayed at a job longer than two years. I want to keep this commitment to *myself* and learn to appreciate the job I have. I'm making the most money I've ever made, and I have the flexibility to take time off when my family needs me. I may not get a bonus, and most people at work don't know me, but I have my own office, and my family is being taken care of.

My relationship with one of my daughters is practically nonexistent, despite the fact that she lives with me. She's gone more than she's home. I've prayed for that relationship to blossom. Don't get me wrong, it used to be worse. There was a time she wouldn't talk to me at all. It was so bad that she didn't allow me to come to the hospital when either of her two kids was born. Today, she lives under my roof, and I get to see my grandkids often. That's progress, and I'm grateful.

My oldest son is moving on with his life. Trusting that God will take care of him is a difficult task. Even though he's alive, God doesn't *owe* me that. Truthfully, when I found out I was pregnant with him, I considered abortion and adoption. But God had different plans. I raised that boy— and now he's 24. It was so hard when my grown kids were little, but I'm grateful for the experience. I wouldn't change a thing.

Last week, I went on a job interview. A client asked me to fill out an application, so I did—without any real intention of leaving my current job. I've now had two interviews. And even though I wasn't looking for a job, now

I can't stop obsessing over what God is going to do next. I've been praying for His will and for the acceptance to handle whatever the answer may be.

Lately, I've been trying hard to shake the feeling of *not having enough.* I've been chasing distractions—energy drinks, shopping, saying I gave it to God, and then taking it right back. Yesterday, I almost spiraled over social media again—some girl commented on my husband's wall. We talked it through. I didn't accuse him, and I honestly don't believe he's cheating on me today. I wasn't even on *his* page—it popped up on my feed.

This couple's church group is helping us. I never thought I'd follow through on something like this, much less believe in its power to help us strengthen our marriage.

I'm learning to run to *God.* And He's showing me all the other "gods" I've been turning to before Him—a new job, new clothes, shopping, even my husband. God will keep letting me learn this lesson until I fully understand: *He is the only One who can fill me.* Everything else leaves me empty. I'll keep being empty until I finally surrender.

Thank You, God, for walking with me—even in the back-and-forth of giving it to You and then taking it back.

Have a great day, my beautiful friend.

Today I'm grateful for:

- I went to church alone on Sunday—my husband and boys were out fishing. But I went anyway. That moment reminded me: My relationship with God is mine—before it belongs to anyone else.
- For *Tuesday's Perspective.*
- To yo*u.*

Are you willing to let God fill the void in your life, or will you keep running to everything else that leaves you empty?

What are you grateful for today?

Grandparents

I found figs at the grocery store on Sunday! They didn't taste quite as good as the ones I grew up eating from my grandparents' garden, but the taste and texture brought back so many memories of two of my favorite people: *my grandparents.*

If you asked me today what my goals in life are, I'd tell you: *to be like them.* They never made money their happiness. They worked hard for everything they had and shared their freshly grown fruits and vegetables from their garden with everyone in the neighborhood.

I remember being about 10 years old, digging up potatoes with my grandpa. He looked at me and said,

"Sister, don't go chasing after what's shiny and new
—or you'll miss out on what you already have."

I replied, "Yes, sir."

My grandmother taught me how to make homemade banana pudding, coconut cream pie, and fig preserves from scratch. One day in my early adult years, I was struggling with what loving someone should look like. I asked her, and she answered,

"Sister, I'll share everything I have to make
sure you've got some too—
but I won't share my husband."

There have been high tides and low tides in my marriage, but my grandparents showed me what love looks like—and how to stay. They taught me to stand firm in what I believe and to be kind while doing so. They taught me how to admit when I'm wrong and that in a fight, nobody wins.

They also taught me how to throw dirt on scraped-up knees and elbows from playing too hard… and to pick myself up when I fall and get back out there and keep playing.

They showed me that having animals is a lifelong responsibility, not just while they're cute. You can't just stop showing up when you're bored or tired. The commitment is for *their* whole life.

Have a blessed day, my friend.

Today I am grateful for:

- That I can look back on the positive lessons I learned growing up, not just the things that went wrong or the mistakes I made. Honestly, all of it has made me who I am today. And I like myself better be*cause of* it.
- I was present when my son found out he didn't make the basketball team. It may have hurt me *m*ore than it hurt him, because he just shrugged and went on with his day.
- For the rain, because I didn't have to straighten my hair after my shower this morning.

What wisdom or memories from your childhood still shape who you are today?

What are you grateful for today?

Grandmothers Advice

Good morning, my friend,

This morning, my husband and I got into a little spat. He's had an attitude for a couple of days, and I'm sure my question this morning didn't help. He left without saying anything, then came back to kiss me—neither of us said, "I love you."

I told myself I wasn't going to put up with any crap today. I was going to ignore him the same way he ignores me when he's frustrated. But then my grandmother's voice popped into my head: *"If you can't say something nice, don't say anything at all."*

Now, I could twist that into an excuse to give my husband the silent treatment—but the more I thought about it, the more I realized what she meant.

On my way to work, my husband texted me to say he was sorry and that he loves me. That's when my grandmother's words sank in. I texted him back, "Thank you for the apology. I'm not going to call right now because I have nothing nice to say. I do love you. Have a great day."

The lesson I remembered from my grandmother wasn't about staying silent to punish someone; it was about pausing before speaking so I don't have to go back and make amends later. It's not okay to ignore my husband, but it *is* OK to be honest about where I am emotionally.

Today I am grateful for:

- The wisdom of my grandmother's voice in my head.
- A husband who's willing to say he's sorry.
- The ability to pause before speaking.

When was the last time you chose silence not out of spite, but out of wisdom?

What are you grateful for today?

Living in the Here and Now

I had a conversation this past week about the way I speak to my children. I caught myself constantly pointing out the wrong things they do, without acknowledging the good things they do. I felt embarrassed and convicted about my behavior as a mother. After that phone call, I immediately asked God to forgive me and help me remember a lesson I'd already learned.

At my previous job, the management constantly criticized me. It took getting my feelings hurt five days a week for six months to realize: I was being treated the same way I was treating my children. How quickly I forget the pain I caused.

But today, I'm thankful God reminded me of that lesson. These past few days, I've made a point to tell my kids the things I love about them, without following it up with criticism.

I also spoke to another woman in my support group about how to help my grown children. She suggested I first ask God what *my* part is and then ask my kids how I can help them, if they even *want* my help. A few days later, I did just that. I asked my daughter if she needed anything and how I could support her. The conversation went well. I felt immense relief from the obsession of trying to fix her life to fit *my* feelings.

Later, I talked to my son on the phone. As he shared his pain, I asked God—right there in the moment—to help me be the kind of mom he needed. I didn't comment. I didn't try to fix it. I just listened. When we hung up, I said out loud during my drive home: *"God, please take care of my children. Protect them. Save them."*

And here's where faith gets tested: Do I trust God with the care of my children? More will be revealed.

My youngest son got into a bit of trouble at school recently. He made fun of a classmate and spread gossip. When the teacher told him he had hurt someone's feelings, my son responded: *"May I call the person I hurt in her class and apologize?"* The teacher said yes. And when he got on the phone, my son told the girl he was sorry for making fun of her and spreading her business around the school—and that he wanted to make it right. After he hung up, he turned to his teacher and said, *"I don't want to be the kind of person who hurts people on purpose."* Even though his behavior wasn't okay, he still took the time to make it right. Proud mama moment.

Today I am grateful for:

- That God is making me a better mom every day.
- For the test af*ter t*he lesson.
- That this recovery process is also reaching my children.

Are you willing to trust God with your children's lives, or will you keep trying to control what only He can handle?

What are you grateful for today?

The Day I Met the Pastel Artist

I met a lady this week who helped me understand what obedience looks like in the middle of fear and doubt. She shared how she became a pastel artist—and how she knows it's God who paints through her.

I've wanted to be a writer for most of my life, not necessarily for money. Some of my dreams involve becoming known because of my writing, but at the heart of it, I want people to know Jesus the way I do. Not the church version of Jesus I once felt judged by. Not the Jesus I was told I wasn't worthy of. But the Jesus who walked with me through my addictions—money, drugs, alcohol, men, people-pleasing, and feeling less than.

The truth is, Jesus never left me. Even in all those moments when I felt the church—or the people in it—were judging me (and maybe they were), that's none of my business. That doesn't mean I didn't care. I did. I *do*. I care deeply about what people think of me. But I'm learning to be myself anyway. The truth is, all along, it was me who was judging myself the most. You could never hate or criticize me more than I already hate or criticize myself. I spent years trying to kill myself slowly, without ever having a suicide plan. If you know what I mean.

The lady, the artist I met, encouraged me to keep writing and to be the woman God made me to be. That one hour with her reopened a door I had recently closed. Why? Because one person told me I wasn't ready to be a writer. And that opinion wounded my pride. It made me question whether I was even capable of helping people or becoming the writer I've always dreamed of being. I didn't even mention it to God. I almost gave up.

Until that artist made something clear: *God is the writer.* And when I ask Him to write through me—if it's His perfect will—then I'm simply being obedient.

I never know who God is going to put in my life. And most of the time, I don't understand the purpose until years later. It's my job to ask God to help me love them, and to see them the way He loves and sees me.

Have an amazing day, my friend. Jesus loves you—and so do I.

Today I am grateful for:

- I'm grateful for the artist God used to reopen a door I had no business closing.
- I'm grateful I don't know what's going to happen with my writing, because I trust God.
- I'm grateful for the grace to be kind to people who have recently hurt me, and to accept that it's not my job to hurt them back.

What doors in your life have you closed because of fear, pride, or someone else's opinion—that God might be asking you to reopen?

What are you grateful for today?

Doctor Visits and the Unknown Doctor

What a week. I went to the doctor and learned that even though I've been taking iron pills, my iron levels are still declining. I have a few tests ahead over the next few weeks. The good news? I'll probably need a hysterectomy. The bad news? I'll probably need a hysterectomy.

The fear creeps in—what will my family do while I recover? How will we pay the bills? Who's going to do my job at work? This is where faith gets put into practice at its best.

One of my children is living what I consider a perilous life. And now I'm having to practice the same powerlessness I once put my own family through. I no longer question why my mom tried so hard to save me so many times.

At work, I've had a few disagreements with my GMs. I even cried in front of my boss—and I've been embarrassed about it ever since. I can't fix my emotions or the situation. Staying committed to both my recovery and this job is *so* uncomfortable. I'm exhausted from trying to figure out how God wants me to handle all of this.

And then, in a calm voice, I hear: *"Be still. I got you."*

I'm still learning how to stay.

I was asked to share the *Traditions* for the next four Wednesdays. I said yes… and immediately wanted to take it back. *What do I even know about the Traditions?* Fear showed up right away.

What if I sound ridiculous when I'm sharing?

What if the doctor says I have cancer after these tests?

What if one of my sons never makes it home?

What if I'm not good enough for this job, and then no one else will hire me?

All these thoughts are my cue: I need to get to a meeting. ASAP.

Thank you for listening. Have an amazing evening.

Today I am grateful for:

- The calm reminders from God that I don't have to figure everything out
- The chance to share, even when I feel unqualified
- Doctors and tests that help uncover the unknown

When fear starts asking "what if," are you willing to pause and listen for God's calm voice instead?

What are you grateful for today?

Boundaries Through the Pain

Saying no is not something I do often—or well. I like to tell people (and even convince myself) that I can say no and stick to it at all costs. Until it costs me my feelings.

Once I start feeling sad about someone else's choices, I cave. I say yes at the expense of my integrity and sanity. I get in the way of myself—and in the way of God.

I've spent a lot of time running in my life. Every time things got bad or didn't go as planned, I'd throw my hands up and walk away. Or I'd scramble to fix it, to change it completely. Half the time, I was left with regret and shame for not following through on my commitments. So much of my life was wasted looking around for the answers instead of looking up.

What would my boundaries look like if I actually followed through? How would I deal with the pain and disappointment that comes from believing I caused something I never had control over in the first place?

I'm facing that pain today—and walking through it with my head held high. No more running back to the past to fix the present. No more trying to validate the kind of person I am based on someone else's decisions.

I love you, my beautiful friend.

Today I'm grateful for:

- For what I continue to learn about myself each day
- For the strength within me that comes from God
- I don't know what the future holds—or have all the answers

Where in your life do you need to stop caving—and trust God to meet you in the discomfort of saying no?

What are you grateful for today?

Not a Cheater Anymore

This past week, I've learned some valuable lessons about who I am now and how I still sometimes compare the old me to the new me. This one is a bit lengthy, but it's worth sharing.

Remember last Tuesday, when I said I wasn't going to share negative things about my husband anymore? Well… I lied.

Over the weekend, my husband and I were at odds. I believed I was right, and he was wrong. In my mind, *he* was the one blowing things out of proportion. So, what did I do? I blew things out of proportion right back.

I met disease with disease.

Not only did I tell ladies in my support group how "wrong" my husband was, but I also posted our dirty laundry on a social media platform chat. I took the post down a few minutes later, but the damage was already done. Responses from my post started pouring in. Calls came quickly.

In that moment, I felt justified. I even felt *proud*, as if I had successfully recruited people to **Team Jennifer**. But almost as quickly as I felt proud, I felt sad and disappointed. Angry at myself for how I'd handled it.

I shared with a woman in my support group that I didn't even understand *why* I'd stayed faithful to one man if this is how things were going to feel. All I wanted in that moment was to feel loved, respected, and heard by my husband.

For eight years, to be exact, I've believed that if my husband made me mad enough, I'd eventually cheat.

But then at a local group's anniversary over the weekend, I saw my ex-boyfriend.

Instead of trying to get his attention (like the old me would've done, especially when hurting over my marriage), I *acted like I didn't even see him*. And my husband wasn't even there.

I was so stressed that if my husband *did* find out we'd spoken—or worse, hugged—he'd be upset. So, I told him.

His response?

**"You should've said hi to your ex and been friendly.
Jennifer, you're not going to cheat on me or yourself.
That's not who you are anymore. So, quit saying it."**

Let that sink in.

Also, at the anniversary, I saw a woman who, last year, told me she didn't like me and asked me to stop texting and calling her. At the time, I was crushed. We had been friends, and I never got closure on why the relationship ended. Back then, I tried everything to get her attention and approval.

But this time?

I saw her. And I ju*st kept walking.*

No chasing. No explaining. No people-pleasing.

Just acceptance.

Later, I told my sponsor what my husband said about my ex-boyfriend being there, and her response was:

**"I agree with your husband.
You've done a lot of work, and you're not a cheater anymore."**

Then she added that she was proud of me for respecting that old friend's boundaries and no longer seeking her approval. That was a powerful compliment—from *two* of the most important people in my life: my husband and my sponsor.

I shared a lot today because I want you to know how *human* I am. I make mistakes. And sometimes I must make those mistakes to grow. No matter how self-righteous or self-centered I can be at times, there is still hope for me.

And growth? It's uncomfortable as hell.

But it's worth it.

Have a great day.

Today I am grateful for:

- Text messages.
- My husband.
- The women who walk with me and don't judge me—even when I'm convinced I'm "right."

What part of your old self are you ready to stop identifying with today?

What are you grateful for today?

Doing the Right Thing Doesn't Always Feel Good

Marriage

A couple of days ago, some of my emotional walls came down. My husband and I went to counseling this past week to work on sharing our feelings and needs with each other—vulnerably and without judgment. We're learning how to fight fair.

Children at Home

My 12-year-old has his first girlfriend. This morning, I asked him to clean his room. He didn't acknowledge my request—he was on the phone with her. I had to tell him to hang up and attend to his responsibilities first. That included cleaning his room before getting back on the phone. These are boundaries I didn't learn until my 40s.

My youngest son forgot to submit his homework, which negatively impacted his grade. I grounded him for a week and explained how important school is—and that his job is to turn things in on time and do his best with every assignment.

Me

Since I didn't go to school growing up, I never really knew how to help with my kids' homework. I didn't know what to check or how to support them. I was too embarrassed to ask anyone for help. My ego, shame, and pride ran the show—and underneath all that was fear. Fear of people finding out that I was dumb and that I didn't go to school.

My older kids, now adults, suffered because of my fear of being honest. Today, my oldest son texted me asking if I could help him with something. He said he doesn't like asking me for things because he has no way of repaying me. I could tell it hurt him even to ask.

I paused. I prayed before I responded. Then I told him, "No." Saying no hurt me deeply.

Doing the right thing doesn't always feel good.

And now, here comes the guilt—the guilt from not helping him with homework nine years ago. This disease of addiction is annoying. No matter how much I've changed or how far I've come, it still finds ways to remind me of all I've done wrong and everything in my past.

Have a beautiful Tuesday!

But today, I am grateful for:

- That God made me a special kind of crazy. I get to be an addict. That fact isn't going anywhere. I can either accept it and feel grateful, or I can sit in sadness over it. Sometimes, both feelings are valid.
- For having an upper respiratory infection and still being able to go to work. Sounds crazy, right? But the truth is—I'm still alive. Whether I'm sick or well, I get to show up.
- For protein and coffee for breakfast.

What part of your past are you ready to stop punishing yourself for?

What are you grateful for today?

Who I Am

My husband and I decided to start counseling with a new therapist to work on my trust issues and his anger.

There are a few situations from when we were separated (before we got married) and shortly after we got back together that I still don't believe he's been candid about. Let me add—we've done counseling before, and these same topics came up. He stuck to the same story then.

(So why would this time be any different?)

I started preparing my list of resentments for our first session. Of course, I wanted the counselor to take my side. And because the counselor is a man, I felt like I needed to convince him that part of me is correct. That fear comes from the possibility of his siding with my husband and dismissing how I feel.

But after some prayer, conversations with my sponsor, and reaching out to a few of my female predecessors and friends, I made a different choice. I decided to make a list of *my own behaviors*—and to ask the counselor how to let go of the past, especially since some of the past might be more *fantasy* than *fact*.

I had to ask myself: What would I do if I *did* hear something new about the past? Honestly, I'd probably hold it against my husband and talk myself into leaving.

(My disease wants me dead, but it'll settle for my misery.)

Does it even matter now—six years later—what did or didn't happen? No. Because I'm not prepared to leave. Do I believe my husband loves me? Yes—with everything in him.

Now that I've walked you through all that, let's get to the *real* issue: The way I'm feeling has less to do with whether my husband is telling the truth… and more to do with the fact that I *still* believe my worth lies in a man.

How dare I give someone that kind of power over me, even if he *is* my husband? I must remember **who I am.** Not what I do for work. Not who I'm married to. Not how many kids I have.

But *who I am.*

I'm kind. I'm mean. I'm thoughtful. I'm selfish.

I'm loving. I'm unloving. I'm compassionate. I'm intolerant.

I'm funny. I'm rude.

And I am God's perfect masterpiece.

I am human.

I am **Jennifer K. Koger.**

In God alone.

Be who you are today—and nothing less.

Today I am grateful for:

- The past.
- The journey.
- The present.

What parts of your identity have you given away that God is asking you to reclaim?

What are you grateful for today?

All About Family

First, I want to express my gratitude to my entire family.

Someone told me this week that my life will get better when I stop being so codependent. I have this habit of trying to fix people's problems.

The acceptance piece?

It's admitting I don't know everything.

It's realizing I have no control over how others act, behave, or live.

What I *do* have control over is praying for tolerance, practicing empathy, and setting boundaries with compassion.

Things at work have been busy, and I've learned that to stay present with the task at hand, I have to actually focus. I can't keep picking up my phone when a family member is in crisis mode. From 8 a.m. to 5 p.m., Monday through Friday, I must attend to my personal affairs, care for the people in my home, and attend to my own needs. Because if I don't… eventually, there will be no one left depending on me at all.

This week, I was able to resolve a conflict with a friend and make amends for *my* part, without jeopardizing the friendship or causing more harm. That's the power of the program.

I also felt under the weather one day at work, and I didn't try to go home. I pushed through because I asked God for help. I don't know about you, but I used to look for *any* excuse to miss work.

But not today.

I sat in the heat on Tuesday and watched my son's football game clean.

Being a mom is worth every minute.

My husband and I don't always see eye to eye. But even in silence, we were on the same page. A good friend once told me, "The way to stay married is not to get divorced." Simplicity.

Tuesday is my favorite day of the week—and here's why:

I've had time to process everything from the weekend.

Monday's catch-up chaos is over.

Wednesday is just the follow-up.

Thursday is for planning.

And Friday? That's when everyone's rushing into the weekend.

But Tuesday? I'm coasting.

Have an amazing rest of the week.

Today I'm grateful for:

- Bleacher seats.
- My sponsor's flexibility.
- A job with a company that was willing to take a chance on an addict like me.

What helps you stay focused on what's in front of you when family distractions pull at your heart?

What are you grateful for today?

Growing Pains

This past week, I stopped by my old job to say hi to my former boss.

Before I got there, I had all these hopeful thoughts—imagining she'd get up from her desk, give me a hug, and we'd have a warm, easy conversation.

But what happened outside of that fantasy—in reality—was very different. She didn't seem happy to see me at all. There was a coldness in her voice, and I felt completely unwelcome.

For days, I thought about calling her to apologize for stopping by unannounced and promising not to do it again. But I didn't call. Why? Because I hadn't done anything wrong. I realized I just wanted to control how she felt about me. That same behavior—trying to manage people's perceptions—bled into the rest of the week.

A friend and I were planning a celebration for our sponsor, and instead of being fully present and focusing on the celebration, I got caught up worrying about two girls who didn't show up. Was it because of me? Was I the reason they stayed home? Honestly, I'm not *that* important to everyone.

I have friends.

Not everything is about me.

On a different note—social media does not have a hold on me anymore. But now, it seems my husband isn't quite ready to log back in to our personal social media accounts.

If I had to guess why, I'd say he's not that different from me. And I'm okay with waiting—because my husband has waited on me before.

These growing pains—around insecurity and social media—have been a process for me for a few years now.

What I've learned is:

Most things really aren't that big of a deal.

It's okay to wait.

It's okay to trust the process.

I'm grateful I get to watch a tree grow.

I don't always notice the changes—until the leaves fall and come back again. And then, one day, that tree has deep roots and offers shade on a hot day.

We do recover. The process is slow. Enjoy the journey.

Have a great day!

Today I am grateful for:

- For coffee protein shakes.
- That today is my son's first tackle football game for school—go school team!
- For the people who showed up to hear me share.

Where in your life are you trying to control how others see you—and what might happen if you let go?

What are you grateful for today?

Seeking Connections with Others

Marriage

My husband and I have been attending a couple's class on Monday nights, and I'm hoping to connect with others through it. I haven't shared that I'm a recovering addict with anyone there yet—not because I'm ashamed, but because I'm still learning how to trust. I've spent so much time judging so-called "Christians" that now, I guess, I assume they'll judge me in return. It's a work in progress—just like me.

Social Media

The social media apps used to have a strong hold on me. I constantly believed my husband was using them to cheat, and I let that belief fester every time he didn't act the way I thought he should. But things are changing. I no longer feel the urge to replace him when I get upset. I'm learning to love him as he is, not as I expect him to be.

Work

I recently attended a breakfast meeting and ran into my former boss. Truth be told, I had been dreading that moment for weeks—I even stressed over what to wear and changed my outfit several times before leaving the house because I didn't like the one I had picked out the night before. I wanted to see her. I wanted her to see how well I'm doing without her—to prove I didn't need her to be okay. But when we finally crossed paths, she was distant. She didn't even hug me. I held it together and acted like a lady, but it hurt.

Still, I'm proud of how I handled it with maturity and grace. I believe God gave me a chance to respond differently in a familiar situation, because He's already taught me that lesson. I sat with my feelings for a while, then thanked God for my current job. And instead of gossiping about my old boss to my support group, I shared how I felt and recognized how both the job and the pain helped shape where I am today.

Friendships

I have some real friends in my life now. For a long time, all I wanted was a genuine connection, but I kept getting rejected, and that was hard. But eventually, I found my people. And let me tell you, people's rejection is God's protection. Today, I've got strong women in my corner who genuinely care.

Feelings

A few women have asked me, "Where's *Tuesday's Perspective?*" And to be honest, I haven't wanted to write. I haven't wanted to see friends, spend time with family, or do anything outside of what's necessary. I've been in a slump.

I no longer take medication to manage my mood, so I've had to walk through this season without a crutch. I'm not mad at myself or anyone else. I'm simply waiting on God to shift something in me. And I know sometimes... that takes time. But I'm grateful.

Today I'm grateful for:

- That when I don't send out *Tuesday's Perspective,* it is missed
- That I can be honest about where I am
- For my relationship with God, and the peace that comes from knowing He's got me—even in this

When you feel insecure, are you willing to trust God to hold you steady—or will you keep trying to control the people and situations around you?

What are you grateful for today?

Perspective in Motion

Good morning, Friend,

I'm off work today because I accidentally booked a large wedding group to have a shuttle on Sunday afternoon and evening.

The funny part? We don't even run a shuttle regularly.

In the past, a mistake like this would have left me feeling resentful, thinking, "It's not my job to drive a shuttle, even if I was the one who caused the situation in the first place."

But today? I'm just grateful. God has changed my perspective—and my behavior.

Today I am grateful:

- that I have a job.
- to have a driver's license.
- that the company I work for trusts me enough to drive their vehicles. I worked hard to get my driver's license back after losing it because of 33 traffic tickets for driving without insurance and with an expired registration… all during my active addiction.

What mistake or inconvenience could you shift into gratitude today, just by changing your perspective?

What are you grateful for today?

Changes

This past week, I filed to have my son's last name legally changed to my husband's—and today was the court hearing. I stood before the judge feeling nervous, excited, uncertain, and overwhelmingly grateful. He asked me, "Do you have your testimony paper ready to read?" I replied, "No, sir! I have no idea what that is."

He looked over the paperwork and told me some forms hadn't been filled out correctly. I stood there quietly—I didn't make excuses or get defensive. Then he asked, "Tell me why you want to change your son's last name." I answered, "Because it's my husband's last name, my last name, and the last name of his younger siblings." We shared a small laugh together, and in that moment, the judge granted the name change. My heart was completely overwhelmed with gratitude.

This is why. My son had carried my maiden name—my father's name. And while my father may have had his reasons, he was absent. I didn't give my son his biological father's last name either—something I'll have to explain to him when he's older. His biological father, who is now deceased, was also absent. Neither of those last names held any meaning in my son's life. But my *husband's* last name? That means something.

My husband was adopted by his dad, and now he calls my son his own, because he has loved and raised him as his own for years. My son made the decision to change his last name, just like he made the decision to call my husband, "Dad."

I'll admit, when the idea of the name change first came up, I didn't believe it would really happen. And when my son was ready to move forward with it, a little fear rose up in me: *What if things don't work out with my husband? What if this ends up being a mistake?* But a friend reminded me today that I can trust God, and trust the process.

I have a beautiful, blended family. I honestly couldn't have asked for a better husband or stepdad/bonus dad for my children. And on top of that—I get to be a stepmom/bonus mom. And you can't tell me these aren't *our* kids. Biological or not, they are all *ours.*

Have an amazing evening, my beautiful friend.

Today I am grateful for:

- That God gave me the understanding to complete the name change paperwork without a lawyer and avoid the extra fees.
- For the women who picked up their phones this week and responded to my texts.
- For a husband who proudly claims both my children and his as our children.

How do you trust God with your family's future instead of letting fear lead the way?

What are you grateful for today?

Letting Go of Yesterday

Yesterday, a family member called and said some hurtful things. I couldn't figure out what I had done to make her so angry with me.

As soon as the call ended, my emotions took me straight back to that little girl inside- the one who felt abandoned so many years ago.

Those feelings bled into my relationship with my husband. I started expecting him to show me just how much he wanted me.

This morning, I woke up carrying the emotional residue from yesterday's phone call. Before I could take it out on my husband for not acting the way I *wanted* him to last night, a friend texted me a video about codependency.

God knew exactly what I needed to hear in that moment—something to help me let go of yesterday's pain.

Today is a new day.

Today I am grateful for:

- The friend who sent a message at just the right time
- The awareness to pause before reacting
- God's faithful presence, even in my emotional mess

What can you let go of today so that you don't carry it into tomorrow?

What are you grateful for today?

Bonus Love

Good morning, Friend,

Today, I get to go on a field trip with my bonus son.

And this time... I don't feel *less than*.

What a relief it is to spend the day *not* comparing myself to other moms. I don't even have to pass judgment on his biological mom for not being here.

Just last week, an opportunity like this would have paralyzed me with fear. I went anyway, with my son. In the past, I would've blamed my absence on anxiety. But the truth is—no matter how I looked on the outside—I didn't feel good enough on the inside to be someone's mom...

Especially not someone's *stepmom*.

Over the past couple of years, I've learned something extraordinary:

My bonus son wa*nts m*e here. He's proud to walk beside me.

I will never replace his mom. But what I want him to know is this:

I love you.

And it's okay to be loved by your mom and *me*.

I call him my bonus son because I don't like how "stepson" sounds. He came with my husband, so he is a bonus.

Today I am grateful for:

- The honor of being loved by my bonus son
- The healing that makes room for confidence
- A heart open enough to love without comparison

What part of your role today once felt impossible but now feels like a gift?

What are you grateful for today?

Still Their Mom

Good morning, my friend.

Being a parent is a full-time, lifelong role.

There's this unspoken assumption that once our kids move out, our job is done. People used to tell me, *"Once they turn 18, you won't have any more say in their lives—so do a good job while they're still little."*

Well … that's not how it worked out for me. I made numerous mistakes along the way. But I've learned that just because I no longer direct my children's lives doesn't mean I stop being their parent.

My role now is to be empathetic. To be emotionally supportive. That doesn't mean I have to agree with all their decisions. What it does mean is—at the end of the day—I love them. No matter what.

Have a great rest of the week.

Today I am grateful for:

- That I still get to be in my children's lives, even as they grow into adulthood.
- The ability to show empathy, not just direction.
- The wisdom I've gained from my mistakes.

What are you grateful for today?

Starting Small

Good morning, Friend,

I don't have much energy today, but I've got *plenty* of ideas on how to fix that.

My first thought? I need to exercise more so I can have more energy. But because that involves actual effort and consistency, my mind immediately jumps to easier options—energy drinks, coffee, and quick fixes.

Today, though, I think I might start small… maybe just a walk around the block. Starting an exercise journey has never been the hard part for me— It's the consistency after *day one* that trips me up.

Have an amazing day.

Today I am grateful for:
- A body that still shows up for me, even when I don't feel like showing up for it
- The wisdom to start small instead of giving up
- The grace to begin again—even if it's for the hundredth time

What are you grateful for today?

Anger and Disrespect

Good morning, Friend,

Today, I'm feeling a little ashamed of how I spoke to several people yesterday while trying to get my son's phone fixed. Every person I talked to transferred me to someone else, and each company blamed the other. Long story short, I didn't get the phone replaced.

And I didn't handle it well.

I let my frustration get the best of me and spoke disrespectfully to multiple people. I went back and apologized for my behavior, and today, I hope to do better.

The irony? My *job* is talking to people and selling hotel rooms. If someone called my work and treated me the way I treated them yesterday, I probably would've hung up on them.

But not one of those customer service reps hung up on me. Each of them showed me grace.

My anger and disrespect didn't help the situation.

All it did was create more pain, primarily for *me*.

I wasn't feeling great yesterday. I was tired and hungry, and I didn't stop to ask myself any of the critical questions before reacting.

Today, I'm praying that every word out of my mouth lifts people and reflects kindness.

Today I am grateful for:

- Grace from strangers who could have treated me the same way I treated them—but didn't.
- The awareness to apologize and the willingness to change.
- A new day to try again—with more compassion and patience.

When you're under pressure, how can you pause long enough to let grace guide your words?

What are you grateful for today?

Grace Over Shame

Good afternoon, Friend,

Yesterday, I had a low tire, so I stopped by a tire shop. Turns out, I had a screw in it. There was a two-hour wait to get it fixed, and I was already at odds with my children and my husband, so I chose to ignore it and just went home.

Today, I had a blowout going 65 miles per hour on a busy highway. But God got us safely to the side of the road.

My oldest son learned how to change a tire just by being on the phone with his stepdad. And in the middle of it all… I wanted to be mad at my husband for my flat tire. Of course I did. I wanted to blame anybody but myself for my car and my responsibilities.

But here's the truth: I'm grateful God loves me enough to hold up a mirror gently so that I can look at *my* part.

Today I am grateful for:

- A safe place to pull over during a scary moment on the road.
- My son learning a life skill through connection, not panic.
- A God who teaches with kindness instead of condemnation.

What situation in your life is God using to show you your part with grace instead of shame?

What are you grateful for today?

Progress Over Patterns

Good morning, Friend,

Yesterday, my husband and I got into a little spat. We were in two separate vehicles but met up for dinner with our three boys. While we were waiting for our food, I caught myself saying something I knew would make my husband mad at our children, to shift his focus away from being angry at *me*.

I'm becoming more aware of the ways I avoid facing issues head-on, especially in our marriage. But this time, once I realized what I was doing, I took accountability. I apologized for my part, we worked through it, and I moved on with my day. That's progress.

There was a time when my husband and I would argue for days, and by the end of it, we'd forget what we were even mad about... until the issue popped back up again later. Today, I'm grateful that I have a choice:

I can argue. Or I can work through it.

Today I am grateful for:

- The awareness to recognize unhealthy patterns
- A marriage that's learning to grow, not just survive
- The ability to choose peace over pride

What old patterns are you ready to release so you can grow in your relationships?

What are you grateful for today?

Wrestling with God

Good morning, Friend,

Today, I'm struggling with the outcome of a situation I have no control over. This morning, I talked to God, *begging* for things to turn out the way I want them to. I'm so overwhelmed by fear about how this might end.

When I get like this, it's a whole roller coaster with God:

First, I pray.

When I don't see results right away, I start begging.

And when I st*ill d*on't see results, I get angry.

I start asking God,

"How could You let this happen?"

I even think, *"If God loves me, He wouldn't allow this."*

And yet… Even though God knows my heart, knows my thoughts, and sees all of it—

He still lets me be where I am.

And He loves me anyway.

Today I am grateful for:

- A God who listens—even when I'm yelling.
- The spiritual freedom to be honest about my doubts.
- Knowing I don't have to have it all figured out to be loved.

What fear are you holding that you need to place back in God's hands?

What are you grateful for today?

Freedom from the Old Me

Good morning, Friend,

Today, I took my son to work and dropped my daughter off at home. Shortly after my grown children got in the car, they started arguing. I used to handle situations like this by yelling at my kids—until they stopped yelling at each other. What that taught them, unfortunately, was that *yelling* is how you communicate.

But today? I didn't yell at them as much. I didn't tell them how to treat each other all the time.

I *did*, however, threaten to drop them both off right there on the side of the road and let them figure out how to get where they needed to go.

And the funny part? I believed I meant it.

Thank goodness they didn't call my bluff—because then I would've had to either follow through (and hurt my feelings), or once again prove to myself that I struggle with integrity, follow-through, and letting my kids face the consequences of their actions.

Freedom from the old me takes work.

So much work.

Today I am grateful for:

- A car full of kids—no matter how loud they get.
- Progress, not perfection.
- A God who meets me in the middle of the mess.

What situation this week reminded me how far I've come—and how far I still want to go?

What are you grateful for today?

Silent and Listen

Good afternoon, Friend,

For years, I've known that *silent* and *listen* have the same letters— And yet, I still couldn't quite manage to do either today. When people talked to me, I'd often be thinking about what I was going to say back, usually interrupting them before they even finished. Why? Because I wanted to be right. Or defend my behavior. Or sound like I had some great wisdom to share.

But today, I've learned how to *listen*—while staying *silent*.

Now, I can respond in a way that lets the other person know I *heard* them.

Learning how to communicate takes work. I don't do it perfectly, and there are still conversations that don't go as productively as I'd like. But the good news? I get a few chances every day to practice listening and staying silent.

Today I am grateful for:

- The chance to practice better communication.
- People who are patient with me as I grow.
- A quiet moment to reflect before I speak.

How can I show someone today that I truly hear them?

What are you grateful for today?

Loving Without Guilt

Good morning, Friend,

Today I'm back at work, already missing my kids and my husband. These feelings aren't new, but what *is* new is that I'm not used to loving in a way that isn't completely self-centered.

I've always loved my children the best I knew how. But wanting to be home with my family and *being* home with them used to be two very different things.

During my active addiction, I only wanted to be home with my kids when I felt guilty about being gone. That mindset has changed so much. Now, I sometimes feel sad that my older children are adults, and my younger ones are growing up so quickly.

I'm so grateful to have the opportunity to live differently today.

I'm not a perfect wife, mom, or grandma, but I *am* someone I'm proud to be. And I value the life God is allowing me to live.

Today I am grateful for:

- The gift of being present.
- The chance to show up for my family—not out of guilt, but love.
- A job that reminds me of why coming home matters.

What's something in your life today that used to feel impossible—but now feels like a gift?

What are you grateful for today?

When I Can't Fix It

Good morning, Friend,

I made it to work today. Even though I'm feeling a little better, it's been a hard morning. My son cried and begged me to stay home—he's feeling nauseous, and I hope that he feels better soon. When he was younger, he'd cry for me, but most of the time it would stop as soon as I stepped out of the room. It felt easier back then, somehow.

Now, he's only about four inches shorter than me and weighs almost as much. Seeing him in pain—looking like a young man but needing his mom—hits differently. When my kids are hurting and I'm powerless to fix it, it reminds me just how much I depend on God. And if I'm being honest, I sometimes get frustrated with God for not healing them fast enough—or in the way *I* think He should.

One minute I'm praying,

"God, please help!"

Next, I'm complaining,

"God, you're not doing it right."

But even when I'm inconsistent, God is good—all the time.

Today I am grateful for:

- The reminder that my children still need me—even as they grow.
- The comfort that God hears my prayers, even when they're messy.
- The strength to show up today, even with a heavy heart.

How do you respond when someone you love is hurting and you can't fix it?

When Love Hurts

Good afternoon, Friend,

Yesterday, I helped a friend move out of their significant other's house—and the truth is, they're *both* my friends. The hard part was watching them separate their lives—his things from hers—piece by piece. I could see the pain in both of their eyes as their world was being torn apart.

I wouldn't even know either of them if I hadn't met my husband, and they've both been a big part of our lives as a couple. Staying neutral and not taking sides was rigid… Because I *don't* want them to separate. And if I'm honest, I have this character defect, this deep need to fix things, especially when someone else's pain starts affecting my world.

I remember when my husband and I broke up before we got married. There was this moment when he met me at a restaurant. We had dinner together, and after we finished eating, he reached across the table and handed me back my house key. I'll never forget how my stomach turned and how I felt like I couldn't breathe—like my body was gasping for air.

That memory is one of the reasons I strive to work through issues with my husband. Because if the relationship is worth saving, I don't want to go through unnecessary pain.

Today I am grateful for:

- The gift of empathy—even when it hurts.
- The growth that comes from heartbreak.
- Relationships that have weathered storms and survived.

What relationship in your life is worth working for—and how can you show up differently to protect it?

What are you grateful for today?

No Backup Plan

Good morning, Friend,

Today has already been *a day,* and here I am at work, just wanting to get home and clean. It's funny how I want to leave one kind of work… to go home and do another. But when I'm cleaning, I'm focusing on what's right in front of me.

I used to count down the hours from work to happy hour. Going home and being present in my kids' lives was *not* high on my to-do list. For a long time, I believed my addiction was just drugs and alcohol. But today, I understand that addiction can take many forms.

Sometimes… she even sounds like me. She uses my voice—makes bad ideas sound like good ones. Right now, I'm working on not going into fight-or-flight mode just because a situation feels unclear.

It wasn't that long ago—just a couple of years—when the moment things felt shaky with my husband, I would start looking for my own place to live. I always had a backup place just waiting for things to go wrong. I didn't walk through problems. I *ran* from them.

But not today. I have no backup plan. There is freedom for me in that.

Today I am grateful for:

- A home I no longer feel the need to run from.
- The clarity that comes from cleaning.
- The strength to stay when things get uncomfortable.

Where in your life have you traded fear for freedom?

What are you grateful for today?

Already in the Solution

Good morning, Friend,

I've spent the past week feeling sorry for myself, focused only on the problem, and struggling to see the solution. When things get uncomfortable in any of my relationships, I tend to act out. I start seeking attention, hoping someone will say just the right thing to make me feel loved.

But here's the growth: I no longer seek out a *man* to fill that need.

This past week, I went to every meeting I could and shared exactly where I was, honestly, openly. And wouldn't you know…the whole time I was desperately looking for a solution, I was already in it.

I'm grateful for that shift in perspective.

Today I am grateful for:

- The ability to be honest, even when I feel messy.
- My recovery community, where I don't have to pretend.
- A God who doesn't need me to have it all together.

When you feel empty or unloved, do you turn to people—or to the tools you've been given in recovery?

What are you grateful for today?

Practicing Participation

Good morning, Friend,

My emotions have been a bit of a roller coaster the past couple of days. For example, I told my husband I wouldn't bring something up… and 20 minutes later, I brought it up—over text. And then I had the nerve to justify my behavior, claiming it was because I'm emotionally attached to situations that I'm powerless over.

The truth is, I want my husband to treat our kids a certain way. And the moment he doesn't do it "right," I get frustrated.

The irony? My husband is currently frustrated with one of our children for not living their life based on his life, the way *he* thinks they should. I've let him take over so I could avoid doing my part as a mom to our grown children.

But this behavior hasn't helped anyone—it's only stunted *my* growth. So today, I'm going to practice showing up and participating in my own life—even when it includes conflict. Because the only way I'll ever learn how to get through conflict… is to go *through* it.

Thank God for my sponsor—and the gift of awareness.

Today I am grateful for:

- My sponsor's guidance and wisdom.
- The ability to recognize my patterns.
- A husband who is on this journey of growth with me.

Where are you avoiding conflict instead of growing through it?

What are you grateful for today?

Choosing Acceptance

Good morning, Friend,

Today, I get to go out and market to some companies—and it's going to hit 105 degrees outside. My oldest son is also out working today, back at his landscaping job. Naturally, I'm worried about him and his health in this heat.

It seems like when I'm worried about one thing, I start focusing on something else, like not trusting my children. It's hard to trust my adult kids sometimes. I feel like they lie to me constantly… and honestly, that may not even be true.

What *is* true is that I'm powerless over my children and whatever situations come up in their lives. What I *can* do is this: No matter what I believe is going on, I don't have to cause them harm.

If I'm being sincere, I spent so many years lying in *my* life that expecting others to tell the truth still feels foreign. So today, I'm choosing acceptance.

I'm grateful that I have friends to share my life with, a family that loves me and that I get to love right back.

Today I am grateful for:

- A job that challenges me to grow.
- My son's work ethic and independence.
- The ability to choose acceptance over control.

What would it look like for you to fully accept the people you love, even when you don't understand their choices?

What are you grateful for today?

When Surrender Leads to Life

Good morning, Friend.

I've slowly stopped sending my daily texts because I feel like I don't have anything good to say. My head's been in this space where I ignore what I'm genuinely feeling and distract myself with unnecessary tasks around the house.

I've accepted my powerlessness over my loved ones, but that doesn't take away the pain or struggle I feel inside. I keep hearing the same question in my head:

> *If I had made better choices, would my children*
> *still be making the choices they make today?*

I know, intellectually, there's no way to know. But emotionally, I still hold myself accountable for their actions. I had a mom who helped me correct my mistakes. And it wasn't until I almost lost my children, several times, to the state that I was finally willing to change. Even then, I had to go through that painful process more times than I'd like to admit before I was truly ready to do something different.

The day I fully surrendered, it was just me and God—alone in my house. And on January 1, 2016, He brought me back from the dead.

Today I am grateful for:

- The gift of a fresh start.
- The healing that comes from honesty.
- The presence of God in my darkest moments.

What weight are you carrying today that God has already offered to lift?

What are you grateful for today?

From Chaos to Peace

Good morning, Friend,

I haven't sent a message in a couple of days because I've been hanging out in my head—honestly, I probably need adult supervision to be alone with the subcommittees that live in there.

Lately, I've been obsessing over the outcomes of all *three* of my grown children's lives. They'll all be at my house this weekend, and I'd be lying if I said I wasn't a little nervous. My adult kids tend to argue, be mean to each other, and act jealous, and watching them brings up memories of the drama I used to cause when I was younger.

The beautiful part? It reminds me how much I genuinely enjoy the peace I have in my life today. What I used to call "boredom," I now recognize as *peace*. And for that shift in perspective, I'm deeply grateful.

Today I am grateful for:

- The inner peace I once feared and now cherish.
- A home where my grown children still gather.
- Growth that allows me to respond, not react.

Where have you mistaken peace for boredom—and how can you embrace the stillness more fully?

What are you grateful for today?

Trusting God's Will

Good morning, Friend.

So many things on my heart this morning. I'm working on accepting other people's decisions.

Today, a family member is going to treatment. I wasn't ready to make changes at her age, but I'm hopeful for her, and I trust that God is working in her life just like He has in mine.

I have a job interview on Monday with another full-service hotel. And I'm choosing to believe that I *am* good enough—because God has changed me from the inside out. Yes, I still have work to do. But what matters most is that I value myself.

Not because of my job title.

Not because of who I know or who I'm married to.

Not because of how many kids I have or the kind of house I live in.

I value myself because my identity is rooted in God.

I'd love your prayers for everything going on in my life and for those around me. But I'm not asking for prayers that I get the job, or that my children never use drugs. I'm asking you to pray for God's will, because His plan is always better than mine.

Today I am grateful for:

- God's timing—even when it doesn't match mine.
- The courage of loved ones seeking recovery.
- Opportunities that remind me of my worth.

Where in your life do you need to surrender control and trust God's plan more fully?

What are you grateful for today?

When Gratitude Comes and Goes

Good evening, Friend.

Today has been one of those days where gratitude came and went. A woman came into my job who had been awake for four days straight at the hospital with her daughter, who may not make it through the night. While I was listening to her story, a gentleman in a wheelchair came up to the front desk. He appeared to be covered in urine. My heart went out to both and their circumstances. In that moment, I felt deeply grateful for the life I have today.

But then, gratitude vanished. I had forgotten to get my husband a cheeseburger when I picked up our food. I *did* get him a meal, just not the cheeseburger he wanted. He immediately got upset, got up from the table, and said he was going to get himself some food. Then he left.

I'm usually pretty patient with him, but today I wasn't. I told him not to talk to me and to leave me alone for the rest of the evening. And then, my mind went straight into, *"Why in the world did I get married in the first place?"*

Now that my emotions have calmed down… I'm grateful again.

Have a great evening.

Today I am grateful for:

- My life.
- Perspective.
- My marriage.

When was the last time your emotions got in the way of your gratitude—and how did you return to it?

What are you grateful for today?

Letting Go of the Expert Role

Good afternoon, Friend,

It's been a few days since I've shared my life with you, so let me catch you up. People still aren't doing things the way I think they should—and it's painful to watch them have their process. Let me start by saying this: I'm grateful that God loves me exactly where I am. I struggle, though, to offer that same grace to others.

For example, nine times out of ten, my grown children don't do things the way I suggest. Then I get my feelings hurt when they choose a different path or ignore my advice and experience. Since my life has gotten better—thanks to God helping me change some of my old, destructive behaviors—I've developed this imaginary belief that I know what's best for everyone and everything.

I convince myself that if someone disagrees with the way *I* think something should be done, they haven't "leveled up" to where I am. Haha! If that doesn't scream silent arrogance, I don't know what does.

Let's take a closer look at what this defect causes:

For starters, it keeps me in denial about the real issue—my**self.**

The truth is, if I'm being honest with you and with myself, I don't know everything. And my way is *not* always the best. In fact, many of my decisions over the years have caused pain to both me and others. Still, I'm working to stay in the solution. To focus on my own journey. Letting go and letting God is still uncomfortable... but I'm doing it, one day at a time.

Today I am grateful for:

- The reminder that I'm not in charge of anyone's process but my own.
- God's grace that meets me right where I am.
- The humility that comes from honest reflection.

Where in your life are you still trying to play the expert, instead of trusting others to find their own way?

What are you grateful for today?

Turning the Focus Outward

Good morning, Friend,

Today, I'm going to focus on where I can be of service to others—from work to home and everything in between. Most mornings, I spend time thinking about what I'm going to wear or what the day holds *for me*. And while I do talk to God almost every morning, it's usually about *me*.

But I know God didn't put us here to live in isolation. He placed us together so we can help and support one another. I want to love God's people the way He loves me.

How are you this morning? I'd love to hear about your day—your thoughts, your pain, your joy, or even your anger. You matter to me, and I want you to know how important you are.

Ask someone about their life today. Listen to what they have to say and try hard not to turn the conversation around to be about you. We can practice this together. Have a great day.

Today I am grateful for:

- The opportunity to love others the way God loves me.
- The awareness to shift my focus outward.
- The people in my life who remind me I'm not alone.

Who can you intentionally show up for today, without making it about you?

What are you grateful for today?

The Birthday Surprise He Didn't See Coming

My husband's birthday is on Monday, and since we both must work that day, I decided to do something special for him tomorrow. I booked a hotel room and made dinner reservations—and he has no idea!

Today, he called me at work and said he had gotten off early and needed to run a few errands. I asked if he could please go to the grocery store and grab what we needed for next week. The only reason I asked him to go was to make sure nothing would get in the way of our surprise plans tomorrow (which again—he still doesn't know about).

While he was at the store, he texted me, letting me know he didn't understand why he had to go grocery shopping and why he couldn't wait until we could go together. When he got home, he was still a little pouty and said, "It's my birthday weekend and I'm doing all this stuff."

He still has no idea what's coming—and he might feel like a little PP head when he realizes I was trying to make it special for him.

Today I am grateful for:

- The ability to surprise the people I love.
- A sense of humor when plans don't look perfect on the outside.
- The joy of seeing someone's face when they realize how loved they are.

When was the last time you realized someone's actions—though inconvenient at first—were actually done out of love?

What are you grateful for today?

Worth Staying For

Good morning, my beautiful friend.

Well, it's Monday and it's time for work. My husband turned 42 today, and, let's say, he's officially over being annoyed with our grocery store trip.

I never knew I wanted someone like my husband until I got to know him. In the beginning, it was mainly physical attraction, and we've had our ups and downs. My husband brings out the best in me—and sometimes the worst. But we grow together, and I honestly couldn't ask for a better stepdad for my children or a better husband for me.

I didn't always feel this way. For a few years, I thought my marriage was going to end because neither of us seemed mature enough to be in a relationship. But so far, I've stuck and stayed—and that's something I never thought I would do.

There was a time I believed I'd always be a liar and a cheater, even after I stopped using drugs. Today, I'm living proof that there is a God, He loves me, and that I'm worth staying committed to one man. I'm learning to treat myself—and others—the way I want to be treated.

Today I am grateful for:

- A marriage that challenges me to grow.
- The healing God has done in my heart.
- The example my husband and I set for our children.

What relationship in your life has taught you the most about who you truly are—and who you can become?

What are you grateful for today?

Faith Over Fear

Good morning, Friend

I've been living in a bit of fantasy the past few days, thinking of all the things that *could* happen while my husband and kids are out of town. To top it off, a family member recently insinuated that I'm a loser because I go to meetings, and that my children are losers because they go with me. I've let that person take up way too much space in my head.

The truth is, their opinion of me or my children does not matter. I know better today. I get the opportunity to speak on "Awakening of the Spirit" at a meeting I'm so grateful to be a part of. I'm facing a couple of fears—mostly around being alone for the next three days—but I'm choosing to give it all to God. I'm allowing this season to grow me.

I get to practice trusting my husband while he's away—not because I have complete control, but because I have full faith. God's got me, no matter what.

Today I am grateful for:

- The opportunity to speak on "Awakening of the Spirit."
- A husband I can choose to trust.
- The faith that carries me through fear.

When someone's opinion tries to shake your peace, how can you shift your focus back to God's truth?

What are you grateful for today?

Full-Circle Moments

Good morning, Friend,

Ah, the joy of being a grandma. Just this morning, I cooked breakfast, cleaned up baby puke, bathed my grandson, and watched him play with the books on my bookshelf. It made me think of the times I spent at my grandparents' house when they would read to me.

I used to steal books—so many books—because I didn't go to school much, and I loved learning. I knew it was wrong, but I did it anyway. I would spend hours trying to understand the world around me. I desperately wanted to be in high school like the other kids. I got so tired of lying and saying my mom was working out of town when the truth was that she was in prison.

It's incredible how watching my grandson play with books brings back so many memories—each one leading to another.

What a journey my life has been so far. And today, I'm so thankful for this moment… and this chapter.

Today I am grateful for:

- Precious time with my grandson.
- The memories my grandparents gave me.
- The lessons I've carried from childhood into today.

What everyday moments in your life have brought back powerful memories?

What are you grateful for today?

Leaning Into Love

Good morning, Friend,

I had a fantastic time with my grandson and daughter this weekend. I spent time reading and learning more about subjects that interest me. I'm also practicing getting back into the school bedtime routine.

I've got all these feelings stirring inside because my husband is going to New York for a football game in December. He works hard and has never taken a guys' trip. I genuinely believe this is an excellent opportunity for him to enjoy being clean and surrounded by other men who share his commitment to marriage.

But there's this insecurity in me—this fear that he'll realize he's happier without me. I know that's probably me deflecting my stuff. Instead of stressing over whether I'm "enough" in my marriage (which is total fantasy), maybe I could lean into love.

Maybe I could show my husband more affection and appreciation. Maybe I'd stop spinning out when things are good, just because I'm not used to it.

Today I am grateful for:

- Sweet memories with my grandson and daughter.
- My husband's hard work and dedication.
- The opportunity to grow in trust and love.

Where in your life could you choose love over fear today?

What are you grateful for today?

A Beautiful Mess

Good morning, Friend,

Today, I acknowledge that I am a good wife, mother, friend, and employee. Yes, I make mistakes—and I don't always give myself credit for what I *am* doing each day to be a better version of me than I was yesterday.

There have been many days when the confident me is in a tug-of-war with the insecure me. But God gets the credit for all of it, because I wouldn't be who I am if I only accepted the negative *or* only the positive.

I am a beautiful mess—and I'm okay with that. God's got me.

Have a great day.

Today I am grateful for:

- The growth I've experienced through God's grace.
- The balance between my strengths and weaknesses.
- The ability to see myself as a work in progress.

What would change if you gave yourself credit for the good you're already doing?

What are you grateful for today?

Waiting Room Faith

Good evening, Friend,

It has been a day. My bonus daughter had her baby today by emergency C-section. I'm at the hospital now, not sure of anything yet. The baby was born four and a half weeks early, and the uncertainty is scary. Not knowing how the baby is doing—and having to wait on a nurse or doctor for an update—is nerve-wracking.

The good news is… I am now a grandma to **two little boys**. I'm so thankful that I get to be present and available today. Even though I'm not my bonus daughter's biological mom, I'm willing to show up for her and her baby, however I can.

I'm writing this from the hospital waiting room in Oklahoma.

Have a great night.

Today I am grateful for:

- The gift of being present for my family in their time of need.
- The safe arrival of my new grandson.
- The opportunity to love my bonus daughter as if she were my own.

When you're faced with uncertainty, how do you find peace while you wait for answers?

What are you grateful for today?

Grace That Comes Full Circle

I received a call early this morning that my new grandson will be with his dad and won't be entering the system. I've been able to be there for my bonus daughter as she feels the pain of her decisions. And instead of blocking her number for cussing and yelling at me, I've been able to relate to her pain and have grace for her. It reminds me of how my mom showed me grace when I didn't make it easy.

I'm starting to understand that none of my past pain was for nothing—because now, I get to use it to be there for others where I'm needed. The wisdom I have comes from God giving me understanding through my experiences.

I'm *thankful* to be an addict in recovery. Because today, I have the *privilege* of walking alongside those who are where I've already been.

Have a perfectly imperfect day.

Today I am grateful for:

- The opportunity to show grace instead of judgment.
- The wisdom that comes from walking through my own struggles.
- The gift of being present for my family during hard times.

How has your past pain equipped you to help someone else today?

What are you grateful for today?

Safe but Still Tender

Good morning, Friend.

Today, my new grandson's dad gets to take him home. The other grandmother told me that if I called her son to check on the baby, he probably wouldn't answer, and that I should only call her. That did hurt my feelings, but he's only 18 and probably doesn't have a clue what to say to me if I did call.

The truth is, I have no control over the situation. I'm not sure I trust that the other grandmother will stay in contact or that we'll get to see my grandson. But God *did* answer my prayers—He placed my grandson in a safe home.

The feelings I'm experiencing might partly be tied to the mom I *used* to be, and all the pain I caused my kids and myself when they were growing up. You would think that after all the Step work and years of being clean and working through recovery, I would have fully forgiven myself for the mother I was back then.

For the most part, I have. But some days are just more challenging than others. I'm so grateful for familiar feelings of pain—because if I can remember how I feel right now, I won't use.

Tell someone you love them today.

Today I am grateful for:

- Knowing my grandson is in a safe home.
- The ability to feel and process my emotions without using.
- God's grace in helping me forgive myself little by little.

How can you choose gratitude even in moments when your heart feels left out?

What are you grateful for today?

Hand Over Control

Good morning, Friend,

Today, I'm still working on this internal emotional aspect of myself. My adult children are suffering from the consequences of their decisions, and the mom in me wants to fix it all; comfort them, tell them not to worry, and take care of everything. But I know the most powerful thing I can do is pray and love them exactly where they are. The logical part of me knows I can't save them from themselves.

Trusting God is something I *must* do—and here's the truth: I must ask God to help me trust Him. I know how to say the words, "I trust You," but to do it, with my whole heart… I need His help.

The growth today is that I'm going to do something for *myself*—go to a meeting—instead of trying to control my adult children's lives.

Have a blessed Tuesday.

Today I am grateful for:

- The wisdom to let go and let God.
- The comfort of prayer when I feel powerless.
- The gift of recovery meetings that refocus my heart and mind.

What would trusting God with your loved ones look like in your own life?

What are you grateful for today?

New Life, New Chapters

Good morning, Friend,

We came home yesterday evening, and I'm feeling so many emotions. Being present in all my children's lives as they each move into a new chapter is a truly precious gift. Who knew that my own life experiences would one day help guide my children, both in what to do and what not to do?

New life brings new adventures: laughter, tears, happiness, pain, worry, and wisdom—all wrapped up in each of us. I am so thankful for the journey.

Today I am grateful for:

- The blessing of witnessing my children's milestones.
- The wisdom gained from both my mistakes and my victories.
- The opportunity to share love and guidance through each new chapter.

How have your life experiences shaped the way you guide and support the next generation?

What are you grateful for today?

Obsession, Boundaries, and Being Okay

I woke up this morning in full-blown obsession about my 9:00 a.m. meeting with my boss. I had the entire conversation played out in my head before my feet even hit the floor. Then the fear kicked in, and I thought, *"Forget her."*

But I know that reaction—it's not coming from the woman I am today. It's the little girl inside of me, still aching for her mother's approval. Still carrying around anger from past experiences with my mom.

My relationship with my boss has gotten complicated. I've tried to pull back—kept things more professional and less personal—but I'm still unsure how to move forward. A good friend reminded me yesterday: *"You can't control how your boss feels or what she thinks of you. Just focus on being you."*

So, that's what I'm trying to do—take that suggestion and live it out today.

This morning, I pulled a character defect card from my step work, and wouldn't you know… it said *Overly Apologetic*. God is always right on time.

I've been fighting off a cold all weekend. I even called the pharmacy to make sure it was safe to take certain medications with my daily prescriptions. That may not seem like a big deal to most people—but for me, it's a huge shift in my thought process. There was a time in my life when I wouldn't have thought twice about what I put in my body—when I didn't care about overdosing or mixing the wrong things.

Today, I do care. I don't ride on the backs of motorcycles anymore, and I absolutely care what I put in my body. Because my life is valuable.

In this moment, I'm not looking for reasons to reject myself or find something I don't like. In this moment… I am okay.

Have a great day!

Today I am grateful for:

- The reminder that my life is valuable.
- Friends who help me see things more clearly.
- God's timing—always perfect, always right on time.

When old fears rise up, are you willing to pause, set boundaries, and remind yourself that you are okay today?

What are you grateful for today?

When the Real Issue Isn't the Issue

Good morning, Friend,

Yesterday at my home group, I listened as people shared about the time they spend together. I allowed my feelings to get hurt because I don't get invited to hang out with the group members.

This morning, I woke up still feeling sorry for myself. So let me look at what's going on—and my part in it. First off, I leave right after the meeting. I don't stay to talk or connect.

The disease of addiction is so sneaky—it'll convince me, in *my voice*, that my home group isn't for me. That's how quickly I start booking new reservations to isolate and act out. The truth? I haven't told anyone that I want to be a part of what they're doing. And the more profound truth? I'm still not sure *what* I want to be a part of.

The feelings I'm having aren't even about not being liked, they're about not being able to take away my grown children's pain. I need to be careful, because my disease will use *every* area of my life to isolate me from my lifeline—my home group. In my heart, I know I'm loved and cared for by the people there. I don't need them to prove that.

Today, I'm facing my feelings and the truth behind them: feeling like I've failed as a mother and wanting control over the outcome. So, I'm turning my children over to God again.

Today I am grateful for:

- A home group that loves me, even when I isolate.
- The awareness to see my part in situations.
- God's patience in helping me let go of control.

Are you willing to stay present long enough to receive the connection you're longing for?

What are you grateful for today?

Anger, Fear, and Letting Go

I've spent the better part of these past seven days trying to manage my emotions, going in and out of anger. I've had to ask God throughout the day to help me forgive and let go. The reason I've been so angry is that I've been carrying around this fear that my husband might cheat on me.

Let me be clear: I *don't* believe my husband has ever cheated on me. My concern is that he *might*.

At first, I thought it was because of past relationships, especially my previous marriage, where I *was* cheated on. But as I dug deeper, I realized most of my fear comes from the person *I* used to be—the one who cheated, who damaged relationships, who didn't think about the people she was hurting. So, I've been asking God to forgive the woman I used to be and to help me catch myself when I start slipping into those old behaviors again.

Last week, I didn't send out my *Tuesday's Perspective* because I dared to reach out to an editor and a publisher to ask if they'd help me publish my book. She kindly turned me down and said this:

> *"It sounds like you are still in the process of finding your new self (that's a good thing) while dismantling the former self and lifestyle. For a book of this type to be helpful to readers—most likely ones you don't know—it needs to come after you've found freedom and victory, not while you're still going through the process. It can be very therapeutic to write about your thoughts and assess situations, so I encourage you to continue doing so—for you, not for others."*

After reading her email, I felt immediately discouraged. I told myself maybe I didn't have what it takes to be a writer. Maybe this wasn't what God wanted for me after all. But even with those thoughts swirling, I still had this deep, unresolved desire to share my words with *whoever* wants to listen. So I brought my concerns to God and asked, *Why did I get turned down?* I didn't get an answer right away. But later that same week, a friend said something that stuck with me:

"That just wasn't the publisher for you."

Could I still be a writer? Of course I could. It also means I don't run away the minute something doesn't go the way I imagined it would. Then—believe it or not—my husband shared with me that he wanted to write a book about parenting. And I felt jealous. I thought, *What if he gets published and no one wants to publish me?* After all, he had received an education. He graduated. He "fits" the part.

That little pity party I threw for myself carried over from my clean date celebration, where I found myself feeling like some people didn't want me at the home group, or didn't think I was important there. But here's what I've learned in the past couple of weeks:

- I have no control over other people.
- I'm not the most important person in anyone's life—except my own.
- Just because one publisher said "no" doesn't mean every publisher will.
- And if my husband writes a book? Good for him. I hope he does it and succeeds.

I'm not leaving my home group. I'm not giving up on my writing or the dream of publishing a book. And I'm not attending that pity party I threw for myself.

Have an amazing day, my beautiful friend.

Today I am grateful for:

- The people who reject me—because sometimes that's God's protection.

- My home group.
- My husband.

Are you willing to let go of fear and trust God with both your past and your future?

What are you grateful for today?

Trusting God with Jealousy and Change

These past seven days have been hard—not because my life is terrible or unbearable—just *hard*. I had been praying for a month about whether or not to change my home group. I was asking what the best option was for both my family and me. The truth is, the only reason I even wanted to switch home groups in the first place was because I was jealous—jealous of other women talking to my husband. I wanted to control how my husband acted.

But God, in His gentle way, revealed the truth to me: the issue wasn't them—it was *me.* He showed me that the best thing for my family, for my recovery, and most importantly, for my *relationship with Him,* was to return to the home group closer to home. When I heard what God was asking of me, I threw a full-blown adult tantrum. I told Him, *"I don't want to switch. I'm fine where I am. The problems in this house are because of my husband's behavior, not mine."*

And again, God gently responded, "This is the change I want you to make." I cried. I felt frustrated. I didn't understand. I even questioned if it was God's voice or just my inner drama stirring things up again. But let me tell you how powerful the God of my understanding is:

The *moment* I switched home groups, even though it was painful and sad and hard, I felt an overwhelming love for the very women I had once been so jealous of. Only God can do that.

Tonight, I have plans to eat dinner with my bonus son's mom and her family so he can spend time with his mother. This is only possible *because of recovery.* Only in recovery could I sit at a table with a woman who had a long relationship—and a sexual history—with my husband and *not* feel jealous or superior. Ego and jealousy will *not* be my side dishes this evening.

Today, I get to live in recovery—not in the fantasy world my disease tries to create.

Have an excellent Tuesday and a grateful week.

Today I am grateful for:

- For the trust I have in my husband.
- That I've remained kind to the women I was once so jealous of— and that some of us are even becoming friends.
- For a God who allows me to walk through this process, and who loves me through every part of it.

Are you willing to let go of control and trust God's direction, even when it doesn't make sense to you?

What are you grateful for today?

Getting Out of My Own Way

Good morning, Friend,

Today, I'm going to do my best to stay out of my way. As a woman, I tend to focus on everything I *think* is wrong in my life—and forget to notice the gifts right in front of me.

Like clockwork, this shows up every month and lasts about a week. And during that time, the people closest to me usually get the worst of it.

Saying I "can't control my emotions" is a tired old excuse—at least, that's how my husband sees it. So today, I think I'll put *myself* in a time-out and hang out with God.

Even though I'm at work, I can still choose to focus on what *I* need to work on, not what my husband or my children could be doing better. I'm going to take that energy and turn it inward. I'll focus on how I speak to others, how I treat them, and especially my tone of voice.

Today I am grateful for:

- The ability to recognize my emotional patterns.
- A God who welcomes me, even in my time-outs.
- A job that gives me a place to practice patience and grace.

What's one way I can redirect my emotions today to create peace instead of chaos?

What are you grateful for today?

Here's What's Been Going On

My middle daughter recently moved in with her two kids, my grandbabies. My granddaughter used to cry whenever she saw me. She didn't want me talking to her or holding her. Any time I picked her up, she would burst into tears and scream for her mom. But lately, when she hears my voice, she *runs* to me and wants me to pick her up. Now she cries when I put her down. There is *so much joy* in being a grandma.

I've shared this before, but my grandmother was one of my favorite people in the world—and I'm so thankful we had her for as long as we did. It means everything to me to now be that person for someone else.

I recently logged back into my personal social media accounts for the first time in almost five years. However, the real test came when my husband logged back into his account. That's where the trust issue lives.

I had this wild idea that if I stayed off social media and he stayed off social media, then he wouldn't cheat on me. Because *that's* where all the danger is, right? The truth is: I have *no control* over my husband or his choices. And the more I try to manage his behavior to meet *my* standard of what's acceptable, the more unmanageable *I* become.

I told him recently, *"We both know what the boundaries are in our marriage. I'm exhausted trying to teach you what's appropriate by my standards. How I behave in this marriage is between me and God. And how you behave is between you and God."*

The thing is—I don't believe my husband has ever cheated on me. But I brought old pain from previous relationships into this marriage without ever fully processing what was *mine* to own and what was *theirs*. There was a time I would go through his phone, check the call logs, track his location—thinking that if I was pretty enough, smart enough, funny enough... if I could prove I could live with or without him, he wouldn't leave me. Learning that I *am enough* has been a long and painful road for me, and for everyone who's walked it with me. Especially my husband.

Healing takes time—not just for the people who hurt me or the ones I've hurt, but for those who are doing life *with* me. They're the truly amazing ones—because even though they didn't cause the damage, they've allowed me to be exactly where I am… and they love me anyway.

Have a fantastic week.

Today I am grateful for:

- My sponsor—it's taken me almost four years to consider her a friend.
- The women who remind me not to give up on life or recovery when it gets hard, because I'm not alone.
- My husband. No matter how bad "Crazy Jennifer" has been—or could still be—he stays.

Are you willing to trust love as it is today, without dragging yesterday's pain into it?

What are you grateful for today?

Staying Out of the God Seat

Sharing

I've had the opportunity to share my story with a group of teenagers and a group of recovering addicts. Each time, I invited God to speak through me, and I only remember cussing once. That's real growth for me.

Control

I'm learning how to walk through the discomfort of not trusting people to do what they've committed to. The control and manipulation that come with trying to make others do what I want are *exhausting*. No amount of knowledge I gain can change someone else's behavior. And the funny thing is—it's *not even my own behavior* I'm trying to control. The outcome belongs to God, not me.

Exercise

For the past couple of weeks, I haven't been motivated to do my Pilates or lift weights. I've felt tired and behind most days. I finally asked God to help me catch up and get moving again—and I did my exercises this morning. It was hard to start again, but I'm glad I did.

Change

There are a few things I'd like to see change in my home group. But that means I have to practice being assertive, kind, and factual—while leaving my opinions and ego at the door. The best way forward is asking God for guidance and resisting the urge to control the outcome or gather people "on my team." We're all on equal ground. Truthfully, on most days, I don't even know what's best for *Jennifer*.

Single Women Friends

I used to believe that single women couldn't be friends with me because I'm married. That belief stemmed from past experiences before recovery. But I was wrong. The single women I'm getting to know today are kind, supportive, and genuinely want what's best for me. They're not trying to break up my marriage or "fix" my situation. I'm grateful God is using these women to help me release judgment on others and myself.

Newcomers

For the past three years, I held onto the belief that newcomers couldn't help me because they hadn't been clean long enough to understand my "crazy." But let me tell you—I was wrong again. So many newcomers in the past couple of months have saved my life with what they've shared—and they don't even know it. I was full of pride and ego, and I'm so grateful God removed me from His seat and placed me right back on equal ground with everyone else. We *can* recover together.

Mom / Grandma

I'm still learning how to be a better mom and grandma. I say "learning" because I often struggle to keep my opinions to myself, especially when it comes to how my grandchildren are being raised.

Staying out of the God seat takes intentional practice. A good friend recently told me how insulted she feels when her mother asks, *"Is your child eating?"* I'm guilty of asking my daughter that exact question—and following it up with, *"When was the last time they had a bath?"*

Starting this week, I'm committing to a new approach. Instead of asking loaded questions, I'll ask my daughter how *she's* doing. And if she chooses to share, I'll listen—with no suggestions or unsolicited advice.

Have a great evening, my friend.

Today I am grateful for:

- The opportunity to love my daughter in a new way.
- The women who share their struggles so I can learn how to be a better parent.
- My single friends and the newcomers, because not only can I listen to them and be their friend, but they've also helped me more than they know.

Are you willing to let God be God—and trust Him with the people you love—instead of trying to control the outcome?

What are you grateful for today?

So, Let's Talk About This Past Week

My husband wanted me to enroll our son in AP classes. When he first suggested it, I immediately became frustrated. I didn't understand why he wanted to put our son in more challenging classes when he was already struggling to improve his grades. My husband explained that our son doesn't study, and that's exactly why he wants more for him. He knows our son *can* handle it. I pleaded my case and told him, "*We are not putting my son in harder classes.*" Yep—*my* son. Because in that moment, he wasn't *our* son. He was *mine.*

I realized I tend to switch to "my son" when I want to get my way, especially when it comes to parenting. That hit me. The truth is, I felt like I was protecting my son from unnecessary pressure. But what I was really protecting… was *my fear.* So, I called a friend. She lovingly reminded me that my husband is teaching our little boy how to be a man—and since I don't know how to teach him those things, I need to trust the man who does. That helped me see things differently. I apologized to my husband, and now we're both encouraging *our* kids to do better in school.

Our son is in the band, and both my husband and I attended his concert this week. It's part of the encouragement process. We're learning how to show up for our kids and each other.   We're also going to a couple's class at church. It's taking me a while to warm up. Why? Because I still spend more time judging church people the way I was once considered by a few so-called "Christians." And the hard truth is—I'm no better than they were to me. I sit around judging people… for judging me. Worse, I hold *other* Christians responsible for how a *few* have treated me. That's not fair. It's not fair to label someone just "a Christian" and forget they're human—just like me.

Thank God people don't label me *only* as an addict. Because that's not all I am. I'm working on treating others the way God treats me. And let's just say—I'm a work in progress.

I'm grateful for school—and even more thankful that my husband had the experience of school growing up, because I didn't. Now he helps our boys with homework, and I get to see the fruit of that experience.

Have a great day, my beautiful friend. I love you to the moon and back—and around my backyard three times.

Today I am grateful for:

- The UIL concert I get to attend today, for our son.
- A job that allows me to come in late and stay late, so I can be present for school events.
- My husband's patience and experience that help shape the boys into young men.

Where are you letting fear disguise itself as protection, instead of trusting God and those He has placed in your life?

What are you grateful for today?

The Other Side of the Fence

Monday, my husband and I seemed to be at odds with each other. As the week progressed, I discovered that I had lost some weight. (Still chasing the lie that my appearance will make me happy.) The significant part, though? I'm taking better care of myself.

My husband went out of town on Friday, and by Saturday evening, we were back to fighting—same argument, different day, over the phone. I really thought I had let go of the past. I wanted to blame my husband for dragging it back into the present. I spent a good part of Saturday night crying and asking God to please protect me… from *me.*

I ended up texting my husband about 50 times—give or take. Sunday morning, I woke up with a stomach full of shame and regret. Thankfully, he's out of town for a week, so I wasn't able to wake up and keep the fight going. The hard part is now I'm left to deal with *myself.*

I apologized to my husband, even though I'm still hurt and frustrated by his behavior. And I had to ask myself: *Will it ever change?* The truth? I don't know. And that's between him and God.

On a more positive note, I haven't looked up my husband's cell phone records or called him repeatedly, even though a part of me feels justified in doing so. I've noticed I'm still putting my worth, security, and happiness in the hands of a man—even if that man is my husband. Marriage is hard.

And letting God work out my relationship is scary. Because deep down, I'm afraid I won't get what I want—or that I'll lose it altogether. When those fears start bubbling up, I distract myself by scrolling through social media platforms. And, of course, it looks like everyone else is doing better than I am. That's my disease—so insidious. It convinces me that the good in my life is small, and the bad is everything.

You know the saying, *"The grass is greener on the other side."* What that saying doesn't tell you is *why* the grass is greener. Here's what I believe: The grass looks greener on the other side because I'm comparing my current situation to someone else's life, without considering how much effort and maintenance went into their lawn. I'm comparing my season to theirs, even though we're in completely different seasons.

What I've come to understand is this: The other side of the fence only *seems* better because they were willing to do the work to keep it maintained. My season will change. And my willingness and actions will determine how I see the growth and color on *my* side of the fence.
I need to do the work and leave the results to God.

Today I am grateful for:

- The reminder that my worth doesn't depend on my husband's behavior or anyone else's approval.
- God's grace that meets me in the middle of my shame and helps me try again.
- The truth that my season will change when I focus on my own growth instead of comparisons.

Are you willing to trust God enough to tend your own side of the fence, even when you can't see the results yet?

What are you grateful for today?

Tug-of-War With God

Someone close to me recently went to jail because of their own actions. My heart broke the moment I found out. Immediately, I started scheming—figuring out how I could help, how much I could afford to bond them out. I told myself I could give up the money I've been saving to start my book. Or forfeit the savings for my much-needed surgery, which is coming up in July. I even thought that *maybe I could get a part-time job to cover whatever I take from those savings.*

But here's the thing…Before this person went to jail, I prayed. I asked God to either put them in jail or save them in whatever way He saw fit. I prayed that prayer because I didn't want this person to die in the streets… or in some stranger's house because of the life they're living.

But the moment fear crept in, I started trying to take it all back. *"Okay, God, I know I asked You to intervene, but I can help! I'll get them out of jail. What if they think I don't love them because I'm not doing anything?"*

I kept pulling back what I had already given to God. And then— gently, lovingly—I felt Him say: *"Kiddo, this is My job. I will protect this person and love them the way I see fit. Sometimes I have to let people face the consequences of their choices. Please stop trying to save them. You're only wearing yourself out. I love them just as much as I love you."*

What God said *should* have brought me comfort. But it didn't— because I don't know the end result. And I don't have any control over it.

Let me also add: I've bailed this person out before. More than once. And if I'm being honest, I think a lot of that was about me not wanting to feel bad.

You've heard the saying, *"The definition of insanity is doing the same thing over and over and expecting a different result."* Yeah… I like to test that theory from time to time. But not today. No more tug-of-war with God—at least for the rest of today. I gave Him all three situations. And I think I'm going to let Him keep them.

Have an amazing day!

Today I am grateful for:

- God's gentle reminders that I don't have to be the savior—because that job is already taken.
- The chance to redirect my energy toward healing, instead of rescuing.
- The peace that comes—little by little—when I leave people in God's hands.

What would it look like if you truly trusted God enough to stop taking back what you've already surrendered?

What are you grateful for today?

Dancing Through the Day

Good morning, Friend,

Funny fact: I like putting on music in the morning on my way to work. One of my favorite songs is in Spanish, and I don't understand much, if any, of what's being said. But it amazes me how, no matter what language we speak or what background we come from, emotions don't have an ethnic background.

Side note: I love to dance—even if I don't always do the moves correctly. The goal isn't perfection—it's having fun while I'm dancing. Today, I'm going to practice dancing in my office and being helpful to others.

Today I am grateful for:

- Music that moves me, even when I don't understand the words.
- The joy of dancing without worrying about getting it right.
- The chance to spread positivity at work today.

Where could you bring more joy into your day by focusing on the fun instead of the perfection?

What are you grateful for today?

Letting Go of the Need to Know

Good morning, Friend,

Today, I am going to embrace the uncertainty of this day. I spend so much time trying to control every detail because I want to feel safe, and I want things to go my way. A risk taker? I tell myself I'm not. But what a relief it is just to let *go.* I can already feel the weight of needing to know everything fall off my shoulders.

The truth is, I take risks all day long, from getting in my car to going to sleep, waking up, and even eating. Maybe it's time I accept that God is in control, and it's more than okay to live in the moment.

Today I am grateful for:

- The peace that comes from trusting God with the unknown.
- Opportunities to live in the present moment.
- The freedom that comes when I release my need to control.

What would change in your life if you stopped needing all the answers before you moved forward?

What are you grateful for today?

PROLOGUE

Keep Going

If you've made it this far, thank you for walking alongside me through these pages. My prayer is that something you've read has reminded you that you are not alone—that your story matters, even when it feels messy, complicated, or unfinished.

Recovery, faith, and life itself are not about perfection. They are about showing up one day at a time, sometimes one moment at a time, and trusting that God is still writing your story. Prayer has carried me through moments I thought I would not survive. Journaling has given me space to process the pain, the joy, the victories, and the setbacks. And talking to others—whether it's a friend, a sponsor, or someone who simply listens— has reminded me that healing doesn't happen in isolation.

If there's anything I want you to take away, it's this: **Don't give up. Don't stop praying. Don't stop writing. Don't stop reaching out.** Even when you don't feel like it's working, even when it feels like no one understands, keep going.

Life is not about having every answer—it's about having the courage to stay in the process. God meets us in the here and now, and He will meet you, too.

So take the next step. Say the next prayer. Write the next word. Make the next call.

And above all, remember—you are loved, you are worth it, and you are never alone.

With Love,
Jennifer Kay Koger

ABOUT THE AUTHOR

Jennifer Kay Koger is a woman of grace, grit, and God-given perspective. A devoted mother, wife, and recovery advocate, she has spent the better part of a decade learning to navigate life with humility, honesty, and healing. Jennifer got clean on January 1, 2016, and since then has embraced the transformative journey of faith, motherhood, and personal growth, one day at a time.

Tuesday's Perspective was born from a simple practice: pausing once a week to reflect. Every Tuesday, Jennifer began writing raw, unfiltered truths about her faith, family, struggles, and victories. These reflections, written in the quiet corners of everyday life, became sacred space, where pain met purpose, and where grace softened every sharp edge.

Her writing is candid and conversational, steeped in vulnerability and hope. Whether she's talking about forgiving her past, parenting through tough seasons, or wrestling with faith in the midst of fear, Jennifer invites readers into her world not as an expert, but as a fellow traveler.

Jennifer lives in Texas with her husband and children, working professionally in the hospitality industry while continuing to serve her local recovery community. Her story is not one of perfection, but of perseverance—and *Tuesday's Perspective* is her love letter to anyone brave enough to keep showing up for themselves, week after week.